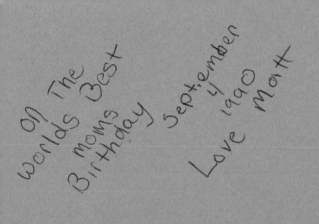

To
worlds Best
moms
Birthday

On The
Best
September
4
1990

Love Matt

CHATEAU STE. MICHELLE

LIBERTY
1886·1986

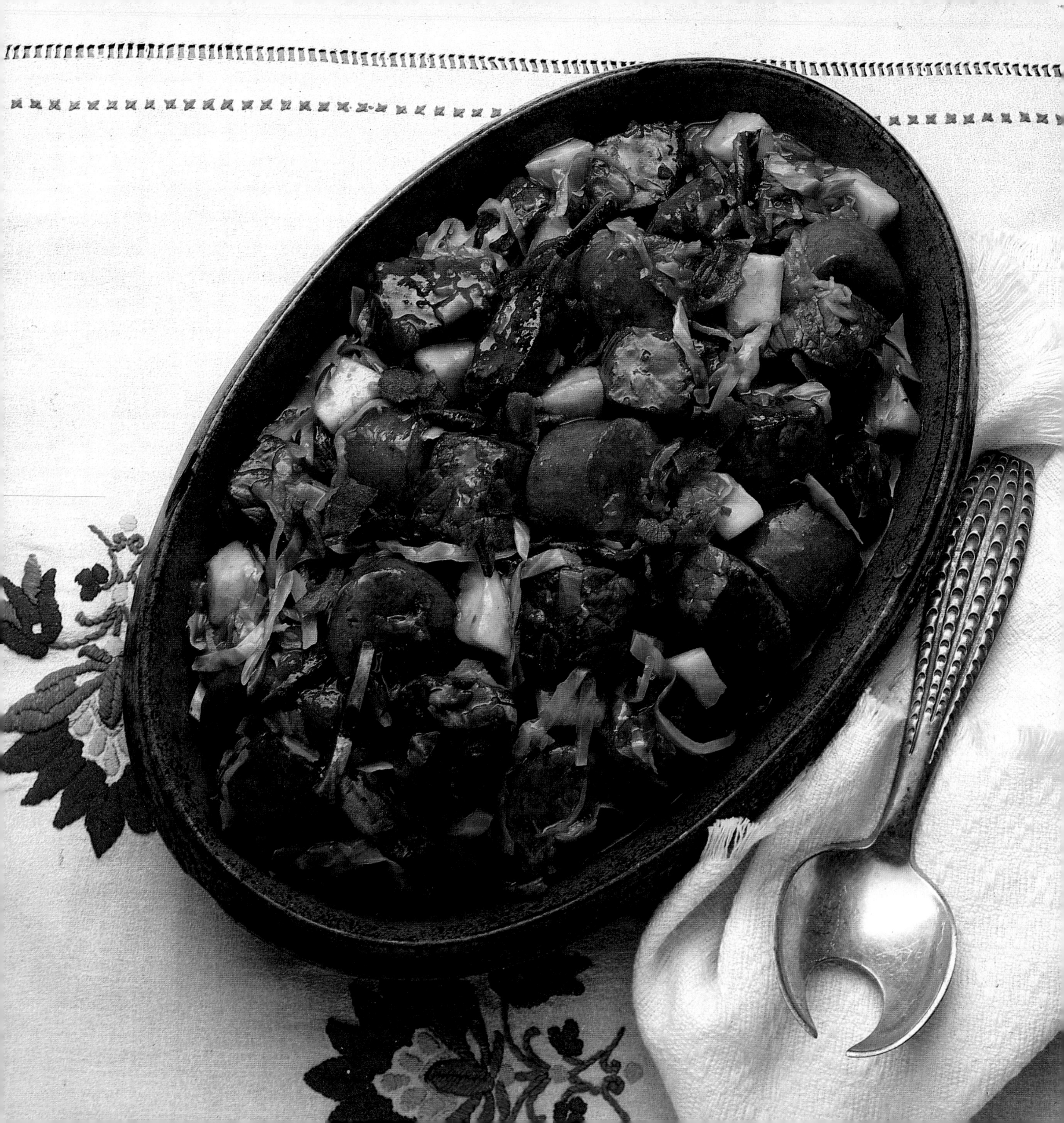

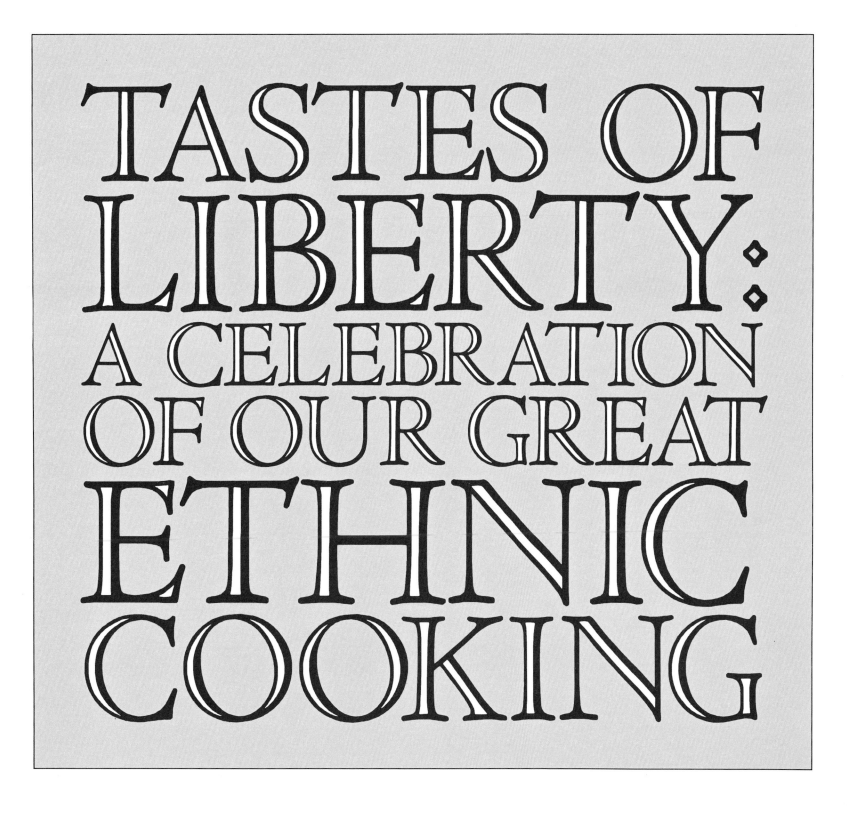

TASTES OF LIBERTY: A CELEBRATION OF OUR GREAT ETHNIC COOKING

Pages 2–3: The Jewish pastry Orechie de Aman.
Frontispiece: Bigos, *Hunter's Stew from Poland.*

Copyright © 1985 Chateau Ste. Michelle
One Stimson Lane, Woodinville, Washington

Produced by Stewart, Tabori & Chang, Inc.
740 Broadway, New York, N.Y. 10003

Library of Congress Cataloging in Publication Data
Main entry under title:

Tastes of liberty.

   Includes index.
   1. Cookery, American. 2. United States—Emigration
and immigration—History. I. Chateau Ste. Michelle
TX715.T2133   1985   641.5973   85-4675
ISBN 0-941434-75-3

Printed in Italy

86 87 88 89 10 9 8 7 6 5 4

Editor: Bob Betz
Design Director: Ted Baseler
Text: Suky Hutton
Recipes: Gail Klatt
Food Photography: Matthew Klein
Chapter Opening Photography: Fred Slavin
Food Stylist: Andrea Swenson
Prop Stylist: Linda Cheverton

Special thanks to:
   Louis F. Bantle
   Lee Iacocca
   Antoinette Iacocca
   Henry Schones
   Allen Shoup
   Edward Jurczenia
   Nicholas Buoniconti
   Sherman Hotchkiss
   Cole & Weber
   Leslie Stoker
   Gordon Harris
   Amla Sanghvi
   Leslie Yoo
   Michelle Siegel
   David Williams
   Thomas O'Grady

Dedication

In early 1983, Chateau Ste. Michelle became a Founding Sponsor of The Statue of Liberty–Ellis Island Foundation, and the first sponsor to direct its efforts to the restoration of Ellis Island. We did so in honor of the island's extraordinary role in American history. During Ellis Island's life as a U.S. immigration station, more than 12 million people surged through its enormous Great Hall, underwent examinations, and in as little as three hours found themselves beginning a new life. Most arrived in the years between 1892 and 1924, before immigration quotas tightened. The cumulative weight of their footsteps wore hollows in the main building's stone stairs.

But bowed steps, testimony to America's magnetism, were followed by far less welcome wear and tear. Ellis Island was abandoned in 1954. For the next eleven years, Atlantic weather, vandals, and pollution battered its buildings. Walls sagged and ceilings fell. In 1965, the island was put in the hands of the National Park Service as part of the Statue of Liberty National Monument. Now, in recognition of the significance of the American immigration movement, The Statue of Liberty–Ellis Island Foundation and the National Park Service together are directing a massive renovation to ensure the preservation of two of America's most important landmarks.

Nearly half of all Americans today have blood relatives who passed through at Ellis Island. At Chateau Ste. Michelle, we feel an additional bond with the history of American immigration; our winery would not exist without the expertise and perseverance that many immigrants brought to the vineyards in their new land. All of our grape varieties originated in Europe, and many of our methods follow time-honored European procedures.

In the spirit of the pioneers who first tested American land, Chateau Ste. Michelle introduced vineyard research to the state of Washington and developed the Columbia Valley, now recognized as one of the very few regions in the world that offers ideal growing conditions. We believe that our internationally acclaimed wines are a classic example of what happens when American resources and European skills come together.

This book is dedicated to the memory of millions of immigrants who brought America a vivid, joyous appreciation of good food and fine wine.

In the heart of Washington's vineyards, Chateau Ste. Michelle's River Ridge winery overlooks the Columbia River.

Preface

Few things about a culture are more personal, or more staunchly protected, than its food. When the English began to colonize America, courteous Indians tried to introduce them to the pleasures of their native fare. Out of necessity, the English accepted—then hastened to import ingredients from home. British food was for them a tangible source of comfort. It looked, smelled and tasted like England, and, together with their religious beliefs and government, helped the colonists feel that they were preserving their national heritage.

The millions of immigrants who followed the English to America had a harder time maintaining their identities. Necessity and desire drove them toward assimilation; they learned a new language, dressed like Americans, lived by American schedules. But in the midst of these radical changes, one inviolable stronghold remained: the immigrant kitchen. When home seemed distant as the moon, nothing was more reassuring than avgolemono, or veal scallopine, or a glass of Johannisberg Riesling.

A slow, steady interchange developed. As the immigrants struggled with English, the language of their food began to speak to the American population. Over time, exotic items such as kielbasa, bagels and bologna slipped past cultural barriers in a subtle promotion of understanding. New cuisines, lively and practical, represented one of the immigrants' gifts to their adopted land.

Chateau Ste. Michelle offers this book as a celebration of the savory results of the melting pot, and of the great relish for food and wine that the immigrants stirred into it. We have focused on the history of nine immigrant groups—why they left home, what they discovered in America, and what they brought to it—in the hope that their stories will deepen your enjoyment of the recipes that follow.

This is a working cookbook. Its recipes are based on well-loved favorites that survived the long trip across the Atlantic, delighted generation after generation, and now give us an immediate, delicious way to explore our heritage. Just as the immigrant felt a bond with the past when he or she sat down to a familiar meal, we can, through a bite of pepparkakor or a sip of Cabernet Sauvignon, travel back through time to experience one of the brightest parts of immigrant life. We invite you to turn the page in the same way that the immigrants approached the new world of America: with an exhilarating sense of possibility.

The French Empire-style Chateau Ste.
Michelle is surrounded by eighty-seven
acres of arboretum-like grounds.

CONTENTS

Italy

Luncheon Menu

Caponata (Cold Eggplant Appetizer)
Fried Mortadella and Mozzarella
Risotto alla Milanese (Rice Milan Style)
Osso Buco (Braised Veal Shanks, Milan Style)
Insalata Verde (Green Salad)
Parmigiano-Reggiano (Cheese) and Grapes
Espresso

RECOMMENDED WINES
Semillon
Chardonnay
Cabernet Sauvignon

Additional Recipes

Pasta e Fagioli (Pasta and Bean Soup)
Zuppa di Pesce (Fish Soup)
Cannelloni (Meat-Stuffed Pasta)
Tagliatelle Ragù (Pasta with Meat Sauce)
Saltimbocca di Pollo
Gnocchi di Patate (Potato Gnocchi)
Raspberry Ice
Crostata di Ricotta (Cheese Pie)

irst came Christopher Columbus, then Amerigo Vespucci. Finally, several centuries later, Italians discovered America en masse. In a wave of immigration unparalleled in U.S. history, almost 4 million *contadini*, or farmers, crossed the ocean blue between 1880 and 1914.

Excitement shines in the faces of newly arrived Italian immigrants at Ellis Island.

Nearly all of them came from southern Italy, with good reason. For centuries, southern Italians suffered a devastating mixture of greed, neglect and prejudice under foreign rule. After Italy's political unification as a nation in 1870, the south, viewed as a poor relation by the new government, was left alone to endure trade wars, epidemics, and a population that increased as relentlessly as Roman taxes. Vineyards shriveled under the assaults of phylloxera and other insects. The *contadini* subsisted on a few pieces of bread dipped in olive oil or on a plate of beans each day. "In Italy," observed one immigrant's daughter, "only the strongest survived."

But as the south battled starvation, a solution emerged. Transatlantic travel became faster and cheaper. Steamships brought with them an irresistible aura of promise: a fresh land, a fresh life. The *contadini* climbed aboard by the thousands, then the hundreds of thousands. They possessed a tenacious but flexible heritage: the ability to adapt to a foreign culture without relinquishing their individuality, their *Italianità*.

Strength radiates from photographs of Italian immigrants at Ellis Island. In one, women in long, full skirts wear scarves, earrings and stoic expressions. Their futures, at that moment, must have felt as shapeless as the bundles they carry, but their eyes blaze with determination.

In another photograph, newly arrived *paesani* (countrymen) all

Dressed in their Sunday best, an Italian family has more than one bundle to look after as they wait to leave Ellis Island, circa 1910.

wear hats, some of them suave fedoras. Their gazes are tough and wary. "We've come to take anything you can dish out," they seem to say. These men have put on their best clothes, suits and high collars, for their entry into America. The fabric is crumpled. The spirit of the gesture is not.

Not surprisingly, no one smiles in these pictures. A member of the United States Immigration Commission, traveling from Italy in 1909, reported that "the atmosphere of the steerage is such that it is a marvel human flesh can endure it." The *contadini* tried to get on deck as much as possible. Some played mandolins or accordions. Women sewed; old men played cards or a finger game called *mora*. Some had more to talk about than others: Guido Gallucci, who made the trip in 1907 at the peak of Italian-American immigration, shared his steerage quarters with 150 passengers and a racehorse owned by a rich American. "The horse was with us while we slept and ate," he recalled. "Ellis Island seemed like paradise when I got there."

Ellis Island was not paradise for most Italians—they named it the *Isola delle Lagrime*, or Island of Tears—and there, as they had throughout their journey, they sought comfort in food from home, sharing cheese and salami, clinging to precious packages of wine, fruit and olive oil. Some had packed cuttings from vineyards at home. Frank Tarallo, who was born on the second floor of a spaghetti processing plant in Little Italy in Middletown, Connecticut, welcomed immigrants at local docks. "I remember all sorts of shouting, greetings and singing to relatives who had arrived . . . the immigrants had to climb the dirt path across the railroad tracks to the customs house where officials checked out the baggages and bundles, which consisted mainly of salami, cheese and onions."

So began life *oltremare*, beyond the sea. Disenchanted with farming, most of the *contadini* turned to commercial or industrial work as the foundation of a new life. They built and maintained railroads; they mined; they sweated in steel mills. In *Old Bread, New Wine*, Patrick Gallo quotes an Italian immigrant: "When I arrived, I learned three things. First, the streets were not paved with gold. Second, the streets were not paved at all. Finally, I was expected to pave them."

A *padrone* system sprang up to supply America's need for strong backs at low wages. Employment agents and labor bosses called *padrones* served as intermediaries between a number of Mediterranean countries and the United States. The *padrone* system was distinguished by its commissaries: Other immigrants might settle for a contractor's food, but the *paesani* demanded their own kitchens.

Italian commissaries, however, stood out as the single bright spot in a grim labor picture. Once again the *contadini* bore the brunt of a chaotic economic situation. On the one hand, America welcomed every sinewy worker she could employ. On the other, she both exploited and reviled a labor force willing to handle the most dangerous, backbreaking jobs for less pay than a native American. By the 1890s American labor forces started to push for restrictions on Italian immigration.

Italian immigrants survived these trials with the resiliency of their ancestors. They drew strength from two things: the family and the re-creation of villages in urban settings—Little Italies. Even as they adjusted to the demands and opportunities of America, they wrapped themselves in the warmth of Italian tradition. Luigi Barzini, in *The Italians*, describes the Italian family as "a spontaneous creation of the national genius, adapted throughout

A taste of the old country is shared at an Italian family supper on the Lower East Side. The photograph was taken in 1914 by Lewis W. Hine.

the centuries to changing conditions, the real foundation of whichever social order prevails.''

Reverence for *la famiglia* spilled over into a great sense of community, where newly arrived *paesani* settled gratefully into the Little Italies that served as buffer zones between their peasant existence and the technological uproar of turn-of-the-century America. In Little Italy, the music of organ grinders and hurdy-gurdies blended with familiar Italian accents. Catholicism among Italians was more exuberant than among Irish-Americans: On festival days, statues of saints, their robes fluttering with money pinned on by the reverent, rode the shoulders of crowds.

At the heart of all Little Italies and their extended families was one inviolate and deeply consoling activity: meals. Gathering with the family around the table was a sustaining event; eating the beloved foods of home enhanced the feeling of security. Italian exporters traded briskly in cheeses, olive oil, canned tomatoes and macaroni; grocers stocked figs, goat's milk, cannoli, lemons and garlic; butchers kept goats for Easter. The *paesani*, hailing from a land Alexis Lichine has described as ''one vast vineyard,'' introduced the custom of taking wine with their meals. ''The Italian,'' says Lichine, ''likes his wines heady, robust and, above all, plentiful. He is the most natural wine drinker in the world.''

Bruna Pieracci remembers the meals her miner father, who immigrated in 1907, cooked for his family in Iowa: ''We were fortunate to have crusty delicious Italian bread brought in from a wagon from another mining camp that had an Italian bakery. It was a bit of Italy in America for them. Some of the miners made their own wine with grapes shipped in from California, and, as the years went on, while they accepted other American ways and things, their food preferences always remained Italian.''

Perhaps because the *paesani* regarded their food with such passion, and because their hearty, rustic style of cooking resembled the native American approach, they exerted a lasting influence on American tastes. Macaroni and cheese, spaghetti with tomato sauce, meatballs, veal scallopine and bologna all became standard American fare. Italy, having introduced ice cream to Europe, doubtless deserves some of the credit in America as well. A New York shop owned by Philip Lenzi in 1777 advertised ice cream that "could be had almost every day." George Washington proved a serious convert: during the summer of 1790, he spent $200 on the Italian dessert that became an American obsession.

Italian-American food is especially characteristic of its people in that it blended into the mainstream of American life without losing its individuality. A picture in Vincenzo Scarpaci's *A Portrait of the Italians in America* says it all. The Gerardi clan is celebrating Thanksgiving in 1950 in Brooklyn. At least 18 family members are seated around a long table, ready for a meal that will include giblet soup, pasta, meat in tomato sauce, yams, cranberry sauce, salad, fruit, nuts and homemade pumpkin and apple pies. On the far end of the table sits a large turkey with dressing. In the center, usurping the spot ordinarily occupied by flowers and candles (or the turkey), sits a flamboyantly iced Italian cake.

Italian workers take a break from building a New York City tunnel, circa 1900.

CAPONATA

Cold Eggplant Appetizer
4 CUPS

1   small eggplant (about 1 pound), pared and cut into 1/2-inch cubes
2   teaspoons coarse salt
1   large red or green bell pepper, seeded and cut into 1-inch dice
1   large yellow bell pepper, seeded and cut into 1-inch dice
1/2   cup coarsely chopped onion
1/4   cup coarsely chopped celery
1/4   cup olive oil
1   1-pound can Italian plum or pear tomatoes, drained and seeded
2   medium zucchini, cut into 1/4-inch slices
2   tablespoons pine nuts
2   tablespoons tomato paste
1   to 2 tablespoons drained capers
2   tablespoons white wine vinegar
1   tablespoon sugar
6   large green olives, pitted and thinly sliced
1   fresh or dried bay leaf
1/8   teaspoon freshly ground black pepper

Place eggplant cubes in colander and sprinkle with salt. Cover with a plate and drain 30 minutes.

Sauté peppers, onion and celery in 2 tablespoons of the oil in large skillet over medium heat, stirring frequently, until onions are soft, 5 to 8 minutes. Remove from skillet and set aside. Add remaining oil to skillet.

Squeeze excess liquid from eggplant. Sauté in skillet over medium heat, stirring frequently, until light brown, 5 to 8 minutes. Return pepper-onion mixture to skillet and stir in all remaining ingredients. Cook over medium-low heat, stirring frequently, until most of the liquid has evaporated, 10 to 15 minutes. Cover and cool to room temperature. Refrigerate at least 2 hours. Remove bay leaf before serving.

FRIED MORTADELLA AND MOZZARELLA

6 TO 8 APPETIZER SERVINGS

Vegetable oil
1/2   pound mozzarella cheese, cut into 3/4-inch cubes
1/4   pound pancetta, cut into 3/4-inch strips
1   cup all-purpose flour
1   cup dry bread crumbs
2   eggs
1   tablespoon milk
1/2   pound mortadella, cut into 3/4-inch cubes

Pour oil into medium saucepan to depth of 1 inch and heat over medium-high heat to 400°F.

Wrap each cheese cube with a pancetta strip and fasten with a wooden pick. Place flour in shallow dish or

Fresh ingredients for the colorful Sicilian appetizer, Caponata.

plate and bread crumbs in similar dish. Beat eggs and milk in small bowl with fork until blended. Dip each mortadella and cheese cube in flour, turning to coat completely. Then dip in egg-milk mixture and roll in bread crumbs to coat completely. Fry about 6 cubes at a time in hot oil just until crumbs are golden, 1 to 2 minutes. Remove with slotted spoon and drain on absorbent paper. Serve immediately.

NOTE: This hot antipasto can be served alone before a meal, with an aperitif or as part of a buffet. In some sections of Italy it is the first course of the grande fritto misto, *a great platter of mixed fried meats, vegetables, cheeses and fruits.*

PASTA E FAGIOLI

Pasta and Bean Soup
6 SERVINGS

1   cup dried Great Northern beans, navy
      beans or white kidney beans
1/2   cup chopped onion
1/3   cup chopped celery
1/3   cup chopped carrot
1/8   pound sliced pancetta or prosciutto,
      chopped
2   cloves garlic, finely chopped
2   tablespoons olive oil
4   cups rich homemade beef broth
1/2   pound smoked pork ribs or neck bones
2   medium tomatoes, peeled, seeded and
      chopped
1   large potato, pared and diced
1/2   teaspoon dried marjoram, crumbled
1/4   teaspoon freshly ground black pepper
1   cup dried ditalini or other small pasta
2   tablespoons chopped fresh parsley

TO SERVE:

Freshly grated Parmesan cheese

Rinse and sort beans. Place in 3-quart saucepan and add enough water to cover by 2 inches. Soak overnight.

Rinse and drain beans, then return to saucepan. Add water to cover beans by 2 inches, then bring to boil over high heat. Reduce heat to medium-low and cook, uncovered, until beans are just tender, 30 to 40 minutes. Drain beans.

Sauté onion, celery, carrot, pancetta and garlic in oil in saucepan over medium heat until vegetables are light brown, 8 to 10 minutes. Blend 1 cup of cooked beans in blender container until smooth, then add to vegetable mixture along with remaining whole beans. Add broth, pork, tomatoes, potato, marjoram and pepper and bring to boil over high heat. Stir in pasta and reduce heat to low. Cover and simmer, stirring occasionally, until pasta is al dente, about 8 to 12 minutes. Discard bones. Stir parsley into soup just before serving. Serve hot, sprinkled with cheese.

RISOTTO ALLA MILANESE

Rice Milan Style
8 SERVINGS

1   *pound fresh asparagus*
     Salt
4 ½ *cups rich homemade chicken broth*
1   *cup chopped onion*
4   *tablespoons unsalted butter*
1   *pound raw Italian Arborio rice*
1   *cup dry white wine*
⅛   *teaspoon powdered saffron*
⅛   *teaspoon freshly ground black pepper*
⅓   *cup freshly grated Parmesan cheese*

TO SERVE:
Freshly grated Parmesan cheese

Wash asparagus and snap off tough ends. Cook in boiling, salted water until crisp-tender. Drain. Cut into ½-inch lengths and set aside.

Heat broth in 2-quart saucepan over medium-high heat to a simmer and hold.

Sauté onion in 2 tablespoons of the butter in large skillet over medium heat until soft, about 5 minutes. Stir in rice and cook, stirring, 3 minutes. Stir in wine and cook until wine evaporates, about 3 minutes.

Dissolve saffron in about 2 tablespoons of the warm broth. Set aside. Gradually stir remaining broth into rice mixture. Stir in saffron mixture and pepper. Continue cooking, uncovered, until rice is tender but al dente, about 15 to 20 minutes. Stir in asparagus during last 5 minutes of cooking. Remove from heat and stir in remaining 2 tablespoons butter and ⅓ cup cheese. Transfer to heated serving bowl. Serve hot, with additional cheese on the side.

INSALATA VERDE

Green Salad
6 SERVINGS

1   *head Bibb lettuce*
1   *small bunch arugula*
½   *head escarole*
½   *head curly chicory or endive*
½   *small head romaine*
2   *medium tomatoes, cut into narrow*
     wedges
1   *celery heart, trimmed and thinly sliced*
1   *small red onion, thinly sliced*
1   *large carrot, coarsely shredded*
1½   *teaspoons finely chopped fresh basil*
     (½ teaspoon dried)
2   *tablespoons fresh lemon juice or white*
     wine vinegar
½   *teaspoon coarse salt*
⅓   *cup olive oil*
     Freshly ground black pepper

OVERLEAF: *Fresh green asparagus is a special addition to the traditional* Risotto alla Milanese.

Wash and trim greens, discarding any bruised leaves. Drain well and pat dry. Tear into bite-sized pieces and place in large serving bowl. Add tomatoes, celery, onion, carrot and basil.

Measure lemon juice and salt into small bowl and mix until salt is dissolved. Stir in oil and immediately pour over vegetables in bowl. Sprinkle with pepper. Toss lightly until vegetables are completely coated. Correct seasoning, if needed. Serve immediately.

OSSO BUCO

Braised Veal Shanks, Milan Style

6 SERVINGS

1   medium onion, *thinly sliced into rings*
1   cup *finely chopped celery*
1   cup *finely chopped carrot*
1   *bay leaf*
4   *tablespoons butter*
1   *teaspoon grated lemon rind*
¼   *cup all-purpose flour*
¼   *teaspoon each freshly ground pepper, dried basil, marjoram and thyme, crumbled*
6   *meaty cross-cut veal shanks (6 to 8 ounces each)*
3   *tablespoons olive oil*
1   *cup dry white wine*
1   *cup rich homemade chicken or beef broth*
1   *1-pound can Italian plum or pear tomatoes, coarsely chopped, with liquid*

FOR GARNISH:

Gremolata (recipe follows)

Sauté onion, celery, carrots and bay leaf in butter until onion is translucent, about 5 minutes. Stir in lemon rind. Remove from heat and set aside. Combine flour with seasonings. Roll meat in seasoned flour and shake off excess. Brown meat on both sides in oil in large Dutch oven with tight-fitting lid over medium-high heat. Add wine and bring to boil. Add broth, reserved vegetables and tomatoes. Return to boil. Cover and place in preheated 375°F. oven. Bake until meat is tender, about 1 hour. Remove bay leaf. Transfer meat to serving platter and keep hot. Over high heat, reduce sauce in pan by one-third, stirring frequently. Pour thickened sauce over meat. Garnish with *Gremolata.*

GREMOLATA

½   *cup chopped fresh parsley*
    Grated rind of 1 lemon

Combine parsley with lemon rind in small bowl.

RIGHT: *A northern Italian classic,* Osso Buco *is enlivened with* gremolata, *a mixture of chopped parsley and grated lemon rind.*
OVERLEAF: *Bright yellow lemon wedges float on a sea of shrimp, clams, lobster and assorted fresh fish in* Zuppa di Pesce.

ZUPPA DI PESCE

Fish Soup
6 SERVINGS

2 tablespoons fresh lemon juice
2 teaspoons salt
1 whole, uncooked lobster or crab (about 1 pound)
1 pound medium shrimp, in the shell
1 pound mussels or clams, in the shell, well scrubbed
1 cup coarsely chopped onion
1 cup coarsely chopped celery, including tops
1 cup dry white wine
2 bay leaves
½ cup finely chopped onion
3 cloves garlic, finely chopped
2 tablespoons olive oil
2 pounds ripe tomatoes, peeled, seeded and chopped
2 tablespoons finely chopped fresh parsley
2 tablespoons tomato paste
2 teaspoons dried basil, crumbled
1 teaspoon dried oregano, crumbled
1 teaspoon dried thyme, crumbled
½ teaspoon freshly ground black pepper
⅛ teaspoon powdered saffron
1½ pounds assorted fresh fish fillets, cleaned, scaled and cut into 1½-inch chunks (use a combination of at least 3 different kinds: halibut, cod, flounder, haddock, snapper, sole, etc.)

FOR GARNISH:

1 lemon, cut into 6 wedges

Heat 4 cups water, lemon juice and 1 teaspoon of the salt to boiling in 5-quart Dutch oven. Drop lobster or crab in and cook 5 minutes. Remove from pot and reserve. Add shrimp to boiling water and cook 1½ minutes. Remove shrimp with slotted spoon, cool with running water and reserve. Add mussels or clams to water and cook until shells open, 4 to 5 minutes. Remove with slotted spoon and reserve.

Add the coarsely chopped onion, celery, ½ cup of the wine and 1 bay leaf to boiling water in pot and reduce heat to medium-low. Cook, uncovered, 15 minutes. Strain mixture, reserving liquid and discarding vegetables.

Sauté the finely chopped onion and garlic in oil in the Dutch oven over medium heat until onion is soft, about 5 minutes. Add reserved liquid, remaining wine, tomatoes, parsley, tomato paste, remaining bay leaf, remaining teaspoon of salt and other seasonings. Reduce heat to low and simmer 30 minutes.

Meanwhile, shell lobster and shrimp. Cut lobster into bite-sized chunks and reserve. Add fresh fish chunks to simmering broth and cook 5 minutes. Add lobster, shrimp and mussels and cook 5 minutes longer. Serve soup hot, garnished with lemon wedges.

CANNELLONI

Meat-Stuffed Pasta
6 TO 8 SERVINGS

Pasta Dough *(recipe follows)*
Tomato Sauce *(recipe follows)*
Béchamel Sauce *(recipe follows)*
3   tablespoons finely chopped onion
1   clove garlic, finely chopped
1   tablespoon olive oil
½   pound lean ground beef
¼   cup dry red wine
1   cup fresh ricotta cheese
¾   cup freshly grated Parmesan cheese
¼   cup freshly grated Romano cheese
2   ounces mortadella, chopped
1   egg
1   tablespoon tomato paste
½   teaspoon dried oregano, crumbled
¼   teaspoon freshly ground black pepper
⅛   teaspoon ground nutmeg
2   teaspoons salt
½   cup shredded mozzarella cheese

First prepare *Pasta Dough*, *Tomato Sauce* and *Béchamel Sauce* and set all aside.

Sauté onion and garlic in oil in large skillet over medium heat until onion is soft, about 3 minutes. Add ground beef and wine and cook, breaking up meat with fork, until meat is cooked through but not brown, about 5 minutes. Remove meat from skillet with slotted spoon and place in medium bowl. Mix in ricotta, ½ cup of the Parmesan, the Romano, ¼ cup of béchamel sauce, mortadella, egg, tomato paste, oreg-ano, pepper and nutmeg. Set aside.

Heat 4 quarts water and salt to boiling in 5-quart Dutch oven over high heat. Roll out pasta dough on lightly floured surface into 20 × 12-inch rectangle and cut into 4 × 3-inch rectangles. Cook 4 pieces at a time, in boiling water until almost done, 30 to 45 seconds. Remove from water immediately and drain on absorbent cloth towels, patting top surfaces dry with another towel.

Coat bottom of greased 13 × 9 × 2-inch baking dish with ¼ cup of toma-to sauce. Spread each pasta strip with 2 tablespoons of meat mixture; roll up and place in dish, folded edge down. Spread remaining tomato sauce evenly over pasta, then spread evenly with remaining béchamel sauce. Sprinkle with mozzarella and remaining ¼ cup Parmesan. Bake in preheated 400°F. oven until golden, 20 to 25 minutes. Let stand at room temperature about 10 minutes before serving.

PASTA DOUGH

1½ cups all-purpose flour
2   large eggs
2   teaspoons milk

Measure flour into mound on large wooden board. Make well in center,

Garnished with a sprig of Italian parsley, Cannelloni *is a classic stuffed pasta.*

place eggs and milk in well and beat with fork. Continue beating eggs in circular motion to incorporate flour gradually into egg mixture, using one hand to support flour on sides of well. When eggs are no longer runny, use fingers to continue mixing until all flour is absorbed. Add more flour, if necessary, to make a dough that is soft but not sticky. On lightly floured board, knead dough 8 to 10 minutes. Pat dough into flattened ball and cover with plastic wrap until ready to roll and shape.

TOMATO SAUCE

1	medium onion, chopped
1	clove garlic, finely chopped
1	tablespoon olive oil
1	1-pound can Italian plum or pear tomatoes
3	tablespoons tomato paste
1½	teaspoons finely chopped fresh basil (½ teaspoon dried)
½	teaspoon finely chopped fresh rosemary (⅛ teaspoon dried and crumbled)
¼	teaspoon salt
⅛	teaspoon freshly ground black pepper

Sauté onion and garlic in oil in medium saucepan over medium heat until onion is soft, about 5 minutes. Remove from heat. Press tomatoes and their liquid through sieve into saucepan, discarding seeds. Stir in remaining ingredients. Heat to boiling. Reduce heat to medium-low and cook, uncovered, 10 to 15 minutes, stirring occasionally. Remove from heat.

BÉCHAMEL SAUCE

4	tablespoons butter
¼	cup all-purpose flour
½	teaspoon salt
⅛	teaspoon freshly ground nutmeg
2	cups light cream

Melt butter in small saucepan over medium heat. Stir in flour, salt and nutmeg. Cook and stir until bubbly. Whisk cream into flour mixture until smooth. Continue cooking and stirring until sauce bubbles for 1 minute. Remove from heat and cover until needed.

TAGLIATELLE RAGÙ

Pasta with Meat Sauce
ABOUT 6 SERVINGS

	Ragù (recipe follows)
2	cups all-purpose flour
3	eggs
1	tablespoon salt
1	cup freshly grated Parmesan cheese

Prepare *Ragù* and keep warm over low heat, stirring occasionally, while preparing tagliatelle.

Measure flour into mound on large

OVERLEAF: *The Bolognese pasta dish,* Tagliatelle Ragù, *features long, flat noodles topped with a richly flavored meat sauce.*

wooden board and make well in center. Place eggs in well and beat with fork. Continue beating eggs in circular motion to incorporate flour gradually into egg mixture, using one hand to support flour on sides of well. When eggs are no longer runny, use fingers to continue mixing until all flour is absorbed. Add more flour, if necessary, to make a dough that is soft but not sticky. On lightly floured board, knead dough 8 to 10 minutes. Divide in half and pat each half into a flattened ball.

On lightly floured surface, roll each dough ball out into a circle 12 to 13 inches in diameter. Carefully roll dough around rolling pin and transfer to a clean towel, spreading out evenly. Let dry at room temperature, uncovered, until dough looks slightly leathery, about 30 minutes. Fold dough over lengthwise into a flat rectangle, about 3 inches wide. Using a sharp knife, cut dough crosswise into pieces 3 inches long by ¼ inch wide. Spread noodles out on clean towel and let dry 5 minutes until firm.

Heat 4 quarts water and salt to boiling in 6-quart (or larger) pot over high heat. Add noodles and stir with wooden spoon until water returns to boil. Cook just until noodles are cooked through, 45 to 60 seconds. Remove from water immediately and drain in colander. Transfer to serving platter and spoon ragù over noodles. Sprinkle with cheese and serve.

RAGÙ

1   medium onion, chopped
2   tablespoons olive oil
³/₄   pound lean ground beef
¼   pound lean ground pork
¼   pound ground veal
1   small carrot, pared and finely chopped
1   small stalk celery, finely chopped
1   cup dry white wine
½   cup milk
⅛   teaspoon ground nutmeg
1   1-pound can Italian plum or pear to-matoes, drained, seeded and chopped
1   cup tomato purée
1   cup rich homemade beef broth
¼   cup tomato paste
2   tablespoons chopped fresh parsley
1   tablespoon finely chopped fresh basil (about ¼ teaspoon dried)
1   teaspoon finely chopped fresh thyme (about ¼ teaspoon dried)
¼   teaspoon freshly ground black pepper
2   bay leaves
½   pound mushrooms, cleaned and sliced

Sauté onion in oil in large skillet over medium heat until soft, about 5 minutes. Add meats and cook, breaking into fine pieces with fork, until cooked but not brown, about 5 minutes. Stir in carrot and celery and cook 2 minutes. Stir in wine and cook until wine evaporates, 8 to 10 minutes. Stir in milk and nutmeg and cook until milk evaporates, about 5 minutes. Remove from heat.

Add all remaining ingredients except mushrooms to meat mixture. Heat to boiling over medium heat. Reduce heat to low and simmer, uncovered, stirring frequently, until sauce is thick, about 45 minutes. Stir in mushrooms and cook 15 minutes longer. Remove and discard bay leaves.

SALTIMBOCCA DI POLLO

4 SERVINGS

3   large whole chicken breasts, boned, skinned and split lengthwise into halves
1/4   cup freshly grated Parmesan cheese
1   tablespoon finely chopped fresh sage
    Freshly ground black pepper
6   ounces prosciutto, thinly sliced
4   tablespoons unsalted butter
1   tablespoon olive oil
2   tablespoons rich homemade chicken broth

Cut chicken pieces crosswise into halves, making 12 pieces. Flatten each by pounding lightly between 2 sheets of waxed paper until about 1/8 inch thick. Sprinkle each piece with 1 teaspoon of the cheese, 1/4 teaspoon of the sage and pepper. Place a slice of prosciutto over each chicken piece. Trim excess prosciutto if desired. Secure prosciutto to each chicken piece with wooden pick.

Heat 2 tablespoons of the butter and the oil in large skillet over medium heat. Add chicken, prosciutto-side up, and cook until golden, 4 to 5 minutes. Turn chicken over and cook until done, about 2 minutes. Place chicken on serving platter. Add stock and remaining butter to skillet and cook, stirring constantly to remove particles from bottom of skillet, until butter melts. Pour butter mixture over chicken and serve at once.

GNOCCHI DI PATATE

Potato Gnocchi
4 TO 6 SERVINGS

2   pounds boiling potatoes
1   tablespoon milk
1   egg
1   tablespoon plus 1/2 teaspoon salt
3/4   to 1 cup all-purpose flour

Pesto (recipe follows)
Freshly grated Parmesan cheese

Place potatoes in 2½-quart saucepan and add water to cover by 1 inch.

Heat to boiling over high heat. Reduce heat to medium-low and cook until potatoes are tender when pierced with a fork, 45 to 55 minutes. Drain and peel potatoes. Mash with milk, egg and ½ teaspoon salt until smooth.

Gradually stir ½ cup of the flour into potatoes until smooth. Sprinkle ¼ cup flour on board. Turn potato mixture onto floured board and knead into dough. (Add more flour, if necessary, to form soft dough.) Shape dough into ropes ¾-inch in diameter and cut crosswise into 1-inch pieces. Flatten each piece slightly with fork, dipping fork frequently in additional flour to prevent sticking.

Heat 3 quarts water and 1 tablespoon salt to boiling in 5-quart Dutch oven. Drop dough, about 18 pieces at a time, into boiling water. Cook until gnocchi rise to top, 2 to 2½ minutes. Remove gnocchi with slotted spoon and drain. Toss lightly with *Pesto* and place in serving dish. Sprinkle with cheese and serve at once.

PESTO

1   *cup cleaned fresh basil, firmly packed*
¼   *cup olive oil*
¼   *cup pine nuts*
2   *large cloves garlic, peeled*
⅓   *cup freshly grated Parmesan cheese*
2   *tablespoons freshly grated Romano cheese*

Combine basil, oil, pine nuts and garlic in blender container. Blend at high speed until smooth, stopping blender frequently to scrape down sides of container. Pour mixture into large bowl and stir in cheeses.

CROSTATA DI RICOTTA

Cheese Pie
12 TO 15 SERVINGS

Sweet Pastry (recipe follows)
1   *pound ricotta cheese*
¼   *cup sugar*
1   *tablespoon all-purpose flour*
1   *teaspoon freshly grated orange rind*
1   *teaspoon vanilla extract*
½   *teaspoon salt*
2   *egg yolks*
¼   *cup golden raisins*
2   *tablespoons diced candied orange rind*
2   *tablespoons diced candied citron*

2   *tablespoons pine nuts*
4   *egg whites*
¼   *teaspoon cream of tartar*

Prepare *Sweet Pastry* and set aside one-third of dough. Roll remaining dough on lightly floured surface into circle about 12 inches in diameter. Fit pastry gently into 9-inch springform pan, pressing evenly over bottom and 1½ inches up sides of pan.

Set aside. Roll remaining one-third dough into rectangle about 10 inches long and cut lengthwise into ½-inch strips. Set aside.

Combine ricotta, sugar, flour, grated orange rind, vanilla, salt and egg yolks in large mixing bowl and beat at medium speed with electric mixer, 5 minutes. Stir in raisins, candied orange rind, citron and pine nuts.

Beat egg whites and cream of tartar in small mixer bowl with clean beaters until stiff but not dry. Set aside ¼ cup of the whites and fold remainder into cheese mixture. Pour cheese mixture into prepared pan. Arrange reserved pastry strips lattice-fashion over filling. Trim and pinch edges. Brush pastry with reserved egg whites.

Bake in preheated 350°F oven until pastry is light brown and filling is firm in center, 50 to 55 minutes. Re-move from oven and cool to room temperature on wire rack. Remove from pan and place on serving plate.

SWEET PASTRY

2¼   cups all-purpose flour
¼   cup sugar
10   tablespoons cold unsalted butter, cut up
2   teaspoons fresh lemon juice
2   egg yolks
2   to 3 tablespoons Marsala or water

Stir flour and sugar together in medium bowl. Cut in butter with pastry blender or 2 knives until mixture resembles coarse cornmeal. Blend together lemon juice, egg yolks and 2 tablespoons Marsala with fork and sprinkle over flour mixture, mixing lightly with fork just until dough begins to stick together. Add more Marsala if necessary and press into ball.

RASPBERRY ICE

6 SERVINGS

2   10-ounce packages frozen raspberries
⅔   cup chilled dry white wine
¼   cup fresh lemon juice
2   tablespoons maraschino liqueur
     (optional)
     Powdered sugar (optional)

FOR GARNISH:

Thin strips lemon rind, twisted into curls

Purée raspberries with wine, lemon juice and liqueur in food processor bowl fitted with metal blade or in blender at high speed. Taste and add powdered sugar if desired. Spoon into individual glass dishes and serve immediately, garnished with lemon rind.

Germany

Dinner Menu

Herring in Wine Sauce
Linsensuppe (Lentil Soup)
Kalter Bohnensalat (Cold Green Bean Salad)
Sauerbraten (Sweet-Sour Marinated Pot Roast)
Kartoffelklössen (Potato Dumplings)
Gurken in Tomatensosse (Cucumbers in Tomato Sauce)
Apfelkuchen (Apple Cake)

RECOMMENDED WINES

Johannisberg Riesling
Gewurztraminer
Merlot

Additional Recipes

Warmer Kartoffelsalat mit Speck (Hot Potato Salad with Bacon)
Hirschbrust (Venison Stew)
Bratwurst
Spätzle (Small Egg Dumplings)
Wiener Schnitzel (Veal Cutlets)
Stollen (German Christmas Bread)
Schwarzwalder Kirchtorte (Black Forest Cherry Cake)

W hen Frederick Law Olmsted, the landscape architect and author, traveled through Texas in the late 1850s, he discovered a remarkable group of settlers. Upon entering one of their homes, he wrote, he was likely to find "a figure in a blue flannel shirt and pendant beard, quoting Tacitus, having in one hand a long pipe, in the other a butcher's knife; Madonnas upon log walls; coffee in tin cups upon Dresden saucers; barrels for seats . . . (and) a Beethoven's symphony on the grand piano." This homesteader, his feet dug into the prairie and his ears tuned to the refinements of music and Roman history, was a German. His countrymen and descendants, characterized by an inimitable mixture of prosaic industry, romantic idealism and conviviality, became one of America's largest ethnic groups.

In the heart of America's dairyland, German cheesemakers pose on the steps of the Swiss Dairy School at the University of Wisconsin in 1923.

According to some historians, the first German to set foot in North America was Tyrker, a shipmate of Leif Ericson, who named the new world Wineland after discovering its abundance of grapes. A few centuries later, Franz Daniel Pastorius, a German lawyer, had the same impression as he led a group of Mennonites to Pennsylvania in 1683 on the "German Mayflower." While founding Germantown, Pastorius wrote home for "a quantity of wine barrels and vats of various sorts," though insects and heavy forests would stymie viticulture.

In the 1700s, German sectarians—Quakers, Baptists (also known as Dunkers), Calvinists, Amish and Moravians—flocked in entire village groups to the tolerant sanctuary of Pennsylvania. Members of Lutheran, Reformed and Catholic congregations came as well from the overpopulated wine-growing regions of southwest Germany. Eventually they spoke the mixture of Ger-

*German immigrants brought with them
their love of sausages, a speciality of this
butcher's establishment.*

man and English that gave them a generic name: Pennsylvania
Dutch.

As many as two-thirds of the German-Americans who arrived
before the Revolution were redemptioners, indentured servants.
Redemptioners signed contracts guaranteeing an average of four
years of labor in exchange for transatlantic passage, then were auc-
tioned off in America by shipping agents. Once their contracts
expired, many developed farms that set the highest standards
along the fertile limestone belt stretching from the Northeast to
the Southwest.

Because the Germans grew grain, rather than cash crops like
tobacco, and because they were stirred by anti-royalist senti-
ments, their fields became the bread basket of the American Revolution. They also supplied the Continental Army with its official
baker, Christopher Ludwig, thousands of soldiers and memorable
leaders, including Baron Steuben, inspector general of the army
and George Washington's trusted adviser. At the close of the war,
only the English outnumbered the Germans in America.

The Napoleonic Wars caused a temporary lull in German immigration. Then Gottfried Duden, a German who had lived on a
farm in Missouri for three years, sailed home and in 1829 wrote a
euphoric book about his experiences. Duden's descriptions were
discussed at the reading clubs common to most villages, while the
nature-loving Germans dreamed of virgin soil, magnificent trees
and fertile fields. The old immigration routes opened once more,
enhanced by improved transportation, and the first of the "Latin
Farmers" streamed into Missouri.

The Latin Farmers gained their nickname because they were
far more at ease with ideas than plows. For many, a fantasy ended
on the frontier of Missouri, where author Duden was dubbed "der

Lügenhund"—the lying dog. German doctors, lawyers and scholars rebounded to St. Louis in search of civilization. Other, hardier immigrants picked up hoes in the morning and books at night. "Their great handicap as pioneers," Richard O'Connor wrote in *The German-Americans*, "was a lingering love of learning." One guest of a Latin Farmer recalled the nights his host tore down rail fences to keep the fire bright enough for reading.

The first peak of nineteenth-century German immigration lasted from 1846 to 1854, when almost 900,000 arrived in the United States, fleeing potato famines, overpopulation and political upheaval. They settled principally in Missouri, Texas and Wisconsin. The last became known as the "German State," producing great quantities of luscious cheeses, expertly made sausages and white-capped oceans of lager. Frederick Weyerhaeuser, lumber baron of the Northwest, started assembling his empire during this period; Margaretha Schurz opened the first kindergarten in America, and an unsung hero named Wendelin Grimm proved he could grow alfalfa in the punishing climate of Minnesota. His strain of clover, named Minnesota Grimm, sank its roots 10 feet into cold clay and far deeper into the history of American farming and ranching.

Also among the first big wave of immigrants were the 48ers, a small but articulate group of liberals. They had experienced democracy during a single year of German provisional government; when it failed, they left for America. Here they persuaded many German-Americans to vote for Abraham Lincoln. German-Americans generally shunned politics as too unstable a profession, but they took forceful stands on certain issues. As a group, they were profoundly anti-slavery: The settlers of Germantown had lodged America's first formal protest against it in 1688.

A German-American butcher demonstrates his skill.

Germans ran saloons like this one in the rough-and-tumble "Devil's Elbow" section of Steven's Point, Wisconsin.

During the Civil War, Germans contributed the greatest proportionate share of soldiers to the Union cause. They also lost the most homesteaders to the Sioux war of 1862. However, the German blend of discipline and quixoticism prevailed: Settlers rebuilt their ravaged farms and a new postwar wave surged forward, inspired by the Homestead Act and the sylvan panoramas painted by artists such as Albert Bierstadt. German-Americans brought the West Conestoga wagons and derringers; they took hold of the Midwestern prairies like Minnesota Grimm, and they founded some of the most famous wineries in California: Krug, Wente and Beringer.

Eighteen eighty-two began the final surge of German immigration. It lasted slightly more than a decade and involved fewer families and more industrial workers. The newcomers joined the largest ethnic minority in America and one of the most quietly productive. German-Americans led the field in engineering, chemicals, optical instruments, agricultural machinery and iron and steel milling, as well as brewing and baking.

They also introduced a cornucopia of wildly varied elements: compulsory gymnastics, postgraduate work, Santa Claus, jelly doughnuts and love of classical music. German-Americans reigned supreme in the orchestras, conservatories and choruses of nineteenth-century America; their pianos rolled to the corners of the frontier, and their choral societies were ubiquitous.

Perhaps the greatest German contribution was *Gemütlichkeit*, relaxed, easy congeniality. The Teutonic insistence on a jolly Sabbath, replete with singing, socializing, beer and wine, scandalized Puritanical Americans at first, but the Germans refused to temper their day of rest. Their influence ultimately helped mellow the national outlook.

"The air is comforting with the fragrance of hops, coffee and tobacco," Ernest L. Meyer wrote, recalling a typical Sunday concert in Milwaukee. "The music fits in with the slumbrous Sabbath feeling that follows a dinner of *knodel* and *sauerbraten*....Waitresses bring trays of coffee and cakes ....Combined with the music of Suppé and Strauss, it induces a benign expansiveness in which one feels like taking the world to one's bosom."

German passengers bid farewell to the fatherland as they leave Bremen on the S.S. Königin Luise *bound for America in 1904.*

HERRING IN WINE SAUCE

8 TO 10 APPETIZER SERVINGS

4   salt herrings (about 1 pound each)
3/4   cup dry white wine
1/2   cup spicy brown mustard
1/2   cup olive oil
1/4   cup white wine vinegar
2   tablespoons sugar
1   teaspoon grated lemon rind
1   tablespoon lemon juice
1/4   teaspoon freshly ground black pepper

Four to six days before serving, freshen herring by rinsing well with cold water. Place in deep glass or stainless steel bowl and cover with cold water. Refrigerate 2 to 3 days, changing water 2 or 3 times a day and rinsing herring well at each change.

Fillet herring and cut into 2-inch pieces. Place in 1-quart glass container with cover. Blend remaining ingredients and pour over herring. Cover and refrigerate 2 to 3 days, stirring occasionally. Serve cold.

LINSENSUPPE

Lentil Soup

8 TO 10 SERVINGS

1   pound dried lentils
1/4   pound sliced bacon, diced
1   large leek, cleaned and chopped, including 2 inches of green top
1   large carrot, pared and chopped
1   stalk celery, with leaves, chopped
1   medium onion, chopped
1   parsnip, pared and chopped
1   small turnip, pared and chopped
1/4   pound smoked pork neck bones
2   tablespoons butter
2   tablespoons all-purpose flour
1   pound bratwurst or frankfurters, cut into 1/4-inch slices
1   to 2 tablespoons cider vinegar
    Salt
    Freshly ground black pepper

Rinse lentils under cold running water and sort carefully, discarding any stones and grit. Heat water to boiling in 5-quart Dutch oven over high heat and add lentils. Return to boil, then reduce heat to low.

Meanwhile, fry bacon in large skillet over medium heat, stirring frequently, until crisp, 5 to 7 minutes. Remove bacon with slotted spoon and reserve. Sauté leek, carrot, celery, onion, parsnip and turnip in bacon drippings, 5 minutes, stirring frequently, and add to lentils. Rinse neck bones under cold running water and add to lentil mixture. Cover and cook 30 minutes, stirring occasionally.

Melt butter in large skillet over

Leeks, carrots, celery, lentils and bratwurst contribute to Linsensuppe.

medium heat and stir in flour. Cook, stirring constantly, until flour begins to brown, about 3 minutes. Pour ½ cup hot lentil mixture into flour mixture and beat with whisk until smooth. Stir into lentil mixture in Dutch oven. Cook, covered, until lentils are tender but not mushy, 15 to 25 minutes longer.

Remove neck bones from soup and discard. Stir in bratwurst and cook until heated through, about 5 minutes. Stir in vinegar. Add salt and pepper to taste. Serve hot.

KALTER BOHNENSALAT

Cold Green Bean Salad
6 SERVINGS

1½ *pounds fresh green beans*
1   *teaspoon salt*
½   *teaspoon dried summer savory,
        crumbled*
¾   *cup rich homemade chicken broth*
4   *to 5 tablespoons olive oil*
3   *tablespoons white or red wine vinegar*
2   *tablespoons lemon juice*
2   *tablespoons finely chopped onion*
1   *teaspoon finely chopped fresh dill*
1   *teaspoon finely chopped fresh parsley*
⅛   *teaspoon freshly ground black pepper*

Trim beans and cut into 2-inch pieces. Heat 8 cups water, salt and savory to boiling in 4- or 5-quart saucepan over high heat. Drop beans into water and return to boil. Reduce heat to medium and cook until beans are crisp-tender, 10 to 15 minutes.

Drain beans and place in large bowl. Combine all remaining ingredients in medium bowl, beat with whisk until well blended and immediately pour over beans. Cover and refrigerate, stirring occasionally, until chilled, at least 2 hours. Drain beans, discarding marinade. Transfer beans to serving bowl. Serve chilled.

SAUERBRATEN

Sweet-Sour Marinated Pot Roast
8 TO 10 SERVINGS

1   *boneless beef rump roast (4 to 5
        pounds), tied with string*
1½ *cups red wine vinegar*
½   *cup dry red wine*
1   *medium onion, chopped*
1   *medium carrot, pared and chopped*
1   *stalk celery with leaves, chopped*

8   *whole black peppercorns*
4   *whole allspice*
4   *whole cloves*
2   *bay leaves*
1   *to 2 ounces suet or 3 tablespoons
        shortening*
1   *marrow bone, cut by butcher into 1- to*

2-inch pieces
1   *medium onion, finely chopped*
1   *stalk celery, finely chopped*
1   *medium carrot, pared and finely chopped*
½   *cup golden raisins*
½   *cup gingersnap crumbs or sour German rye bread crumbs*

Place beef in deep glass, earthenware or stainless steel bowl. Combine vinegar, ½ cup water, wine, 1 onion, 1 carrot, 1 stalk celery and spices in medium saucepan and heat to boiling over high heat. Pour over meat, turning to coat all sides. Cover and refrigerate 2 to 3 days, turning meat several times each day.

Three to four hours before serving, drain meat, reserving marinade, and pat dry with paper towels. Melt suet in large saucepan over medium heat. Add meat and marrow bones and brown on all sides, turning frequent-

ly, about 30 minutes. Remove meat and bones from pan and reserve. Pour off all but 2 tablespoons fat. Sauté remaining onion, celery and carrot in fat until tender, about 10 minutes. Return meat and bones to pan and add raisins. Strain marinade into pan, discarding marinade vegetables. Reduce heat to low and simmer, covered, until meat is tender, 2½ to 3 hours.

Remove meat and keep warm. Discard marrow bones. Pour liquid from pan into 1-quart container and skim off fat. Purée liquid in blender or food processor and strain into pan. Add crumbs to liquid. Heat to boiling over high heat and boil, stirring frequently, until sauce is reduced and thickened, 8 to 10 minutes.

Remove string from meat. Slice and arrange meat on heated serving platter. Serve hot with thickened sauce.

KARTOFFELKLÖSSEN

Potato Dumplings
4 DOZEN

3   *teaspoons salt*
3   *pounds potatoes, pared and quartered*
3   *eggs, beaten*
½   *cup regular farina*
½   *cup all-purpose flour*
¼   *teaspoon freshly grated nutmeg*
     All-purpose flour, if needed
4   *tablespoons butter*
1   *cup fine dry bread crumbs*

¼   *cup chopped fresh parsley*

Heat 3 quarts water and 1 teaspoon of the salt in 5-quart Dutch oven over medium-high heat. Add potatoes and cook until tender, 15 to 20 minutes. Drain and put through potato ricer or food mill. Spread on platter or baking sheet to cool slightly.

Beat together eggs, farina, flour, 1 teaspoon salt and nutmeg in large bowl and beat in potatoes. Shape potato mixture into balls, using a level measuring tablespoonful for each. Place on baking sheet and cover loosely with plastic wrap.

Heat 3 quarts water and remaining 1 teaspoon salt to boiling in 5-quart Dutch oven over medium-high heat. Reduce heat to medium. Place a test dumpling in water and simmer until firm and hot in center, 10 to 12 minutes. (If dumpling falls apart during first few minutes of cooking, stir additional 2 to 4 tablespoons flour into dough.) Cook dumplings, about a dozen at a time, in boiling water until firm and hot in center but still smooth on outside, 10 to 12 minutes. Do not overcook or dumplings will fall apart.

Remove dumplings from water with slotted spoon and drain on paper towels. Transfer to heated serving platter, cover with foil and keep warm in 225°F. oven while cooking remaining dumplings.

Melt butter in large skillet over medium-high heat and stir in bread crumbs. Cook, stirring frequently, until crumbs are golden, 4 to 5 minutes. Spoon crumbs over cooked dumplings. Sprinkle with parsley. Serve hot.

GURKEN IN TOMATENSOSSE

Cucumbers in Tomato Sauce
4 TO 6 SERVINGS

4	*medium cucumbers (about 2 pounds)*
1	*teaspoon salt*
4	*slices bacon, minced*
1	*small onion, finely chopped*
2	*medium tomatoes, peeled, seeded and chopped*
2	*tablespoons tomato paste*
2	*tablespoons chopped fresh parsley*
1/8	*teaspoon freshly ground white pepper*
2	*tablespoons grated Gruyère or Swiss cheese*

Pare cucumbers, cut lengthwise into halves and remove seeds. Slice crosswise into 1-inch pieces and place in large bowl. Sprinkle with salt and cover with heavy plate. Let stand 30 minutes. Drain and pat dry with paper towels.

Fry bacon in large skillet over high heat until soft, stirring to separate pieces, about 2 minutes. Add cucumbers and sauté, stirring frequently, until light brown on all sides, 10 to 12 minutes. Remove cucumbers and bacon from skillet with slotted spoon and reserve. Add onion to pan drippings and cook until soft, about 3 minutes. Stir in tomatoes, tomato paste, 1 tablespoon of the parsley and pepper. Reduce heat to low and simmer, uncovered, until tomatoes are soft, about 10 minutes.

Return cucumbers to skillet and cook until heated through, 3 to 5 minutes longer. Stir in cheese and cook 1 minute longer. Transfer to heated serving bowl and sprinkle with remaining parsley. Serve hot.

German families spice up the humble cucumber by serving it in a zesty tomato and onion sauce.

APFELKUCHEN

Apple Cake
1 CAKE

2   cups all-purpose flour
¾   cup sugar
2   teaspoons grated lemon rind
¼   teaspoon salt
8   tablespoons unsalted butter, chilled
2   egg yolks
¼   cup fine dry bread crumbs
1½   pounds tart cooking apples
1   teaspoon ground cinnamon
½   cup heavy cream
1   egg

Stir flour, ¼ cup of the sugar, lemon rind and salt together in large bowl. Cut in butter with pastry blender or two knives until mixture resembles coarse crumbs. Blend egg yolks and 3 tablespoons water in small bowl and drizzle over flour mixture. Mix just until dough holds together, adding more water as necessary. Shape into ball, cover with plastic wrap and re-frigerate 30 minutes.

Pat dough evenly over bottom and 1 inch up sides of 9-inch springform pan. Sprinkle evenly with bread crumbs. Pare and core apples, cut into ¼-inch slices and arrange over dough in pan. Combine ¼ cup sugar and cinnamon and sprinkle evenly over apples. Bake in preheated 350°F. oven for 20 minutes.

Beat cream, remaining sugar and egg together in small bowl until blended. Pour over partially baked cake. Return cake to oven and con-tinue baking until knife inserted in center of cream mixture comes out clean, about 20 to 25 minutes longer.

Remove from oven and cool cake completely on wire rack before re-moving sides of pan. Cut into wedges to serve.

WARMER
KARTOFFELSALAT
MIT SPECK

Hot Potato Salad with Bacon
6 TO 8 SERVINGS

2   pounds medium boiling potatoes
½   pound sliced bacon, diced
1   medium onion, finely chopped
½   cup cider vinegar
½   cup rich homemade beef broth
1   teaspoon sugar
½   teaspoon salt
¼   teaspoon freshly ground black pepper
1   egg yolk

No German-American family reunion would be complete without Warmer Kartoffelsalat Mit Speck.

TO SERVE:

2   tablespoons fresh parsley, finely chopped

Place potatoes in 3- or 4-quart saucepan and add water to cover by 1 inch. Heat to boiling over medium-high heat. Reduce heat to medium-low and cook until potatoes are tender, 30 to 35 minutes. Drain and let stand 10 minutes. Pare potatoes, cut into ⅛-inch slices and place in large serving bowl. Cover to keep hot.

Cook bacon in large skillet over medium heat, stirring frequently, until crisp, 5 to 7 minutes. Remove from skillet with slotted spoon and sprinkle over potatoes. Discard all but 3 tablespoons bacon drippings from skillet. Add onion to drippings and cook, stirring frequently, until soft, about 5 minutes. Stir in vinegar, broth, sugar, salt and pepper and heat to boiling. Blend about ¼ cup hot vinegar mixture with egg yolk in small bowl and blend yolk mixture into vinegar mixture in skillet. Cook 1 minute and remove from heat.

Pour hot vinegar mixture over potatoes and toss lightly until thoroughly mixed. Serve hot or cool to room temperature. Sprinkle with parsley before serving.

HIRSCHBRUST

Venison Stew

6 SERVINGS

2   cups dry red wine
½   cup chopped celery tops, including leaves
4   tablespoons vegetable oil
2   tablespoons chopped fresh parsley
1   teaspoon sugar
½   teaspoon dried rosemary, crumbled
½   teaspoon dried marjoram, crumbled
½   teaspoon dried thyme, crumbled
10   whole peppercorns
5   whole juniper berries
3   whole cloves
1   bay leaf
3   pounds boneless venison shoulder, cut into 1½-inch cubes
2   tablespoons bacon drippings
2   large onions, cut into ¼-inch slices
2   large carrots, pared and shredded
1   pound fresh mushrooms, cleaned and sliced
2   tablespoons all-purpose flour
1½   cups rich homemade beef broth
1   teaspoon salt
½   teaspoon freshly ground black pepper

Heat wine, celery, 2 tablespoons of the oil, 1 tablespoon of the parsley, sugar, rosemary, marjoram, thyme, peppercorns, juniper berries, cloves and bay leaf to boiling in 1½-quart saucepan over high heat. Remove from heat and cool to room temperature.

Place venison in large glass bowl and pour wine marinade over. Cover

This Hirschbrust, or venison stew, is served in a German pewter tureen from the 1830s.

with plastic wrap and refrigerate about 24 hours, stirring occasionally.

Remove meat from marinade. Strain and reserve marinade. Pat meat dry with paper towels. Cook half the venison in remaining 2 tablespoons oil and bacon drippings in large skillet over medium-high heat. Stir frequently, until browned on all sides, about 10 minutes. Remove from skillet with slotted spoon and reserve. Repeat with remaining venison.

Reduce heat to medium. Add onions, carrots and mushrooms to skillet. Cook, stirring frequently, until onions begin to soften, about 5 minutes. Sprinkle flour over vegetable mixture and cook, 3 minutes, stirring constantly.

Return venison to skillet and add reserved marinade, stock, remaining 1 tablespoon parsley, salt and pepper. Heat to boiling over medium-high heat. Reduce heat to low. Partially cover and simmer, stirring occasionally, until venison is tender, about 1½ hours. Serve hot.

BRATWURST

4 POUNDS

Natural hog casings
3 *pounds boneless pork shoulder or Boston butt, coarsely ground*
1 *pound lean boneless veal shoulder, coarsely ground*
2 *ounces pork fat, cut into ½-inch cubes*
1½ *teaspoons salt*
1½ *teaspoons ground coriander*
1½ *teaspoons freshly ground white pepper*
1 *teaspoon dry mustard*
½ *teaspoon caraway seeds*
½ *teaspoon dried marjoram, crumbled*
¼ *teaspoon ground nutmeg*

Rinse casings under warm running water. Place in small bowl, cover with warm water and let stand 10 minutes. Insert 2 fingers into one end of each casing, hold under warm running water and let water run through casing.

Tie knot in one end of each casing, place on paper towels and reserve.

Grind meats and pork fat together using fine blade of food grinder, or process in food processor fitted with steel blade. Transfer to large bowl and add ½ cup cold water and all remaining ingredients. Mix thoroughly with hands. (If using food processor, add all ingredients to ground meat mixture in work bowl and process, using on/off technique, until well mixed, 10 to 15 seconds.)

To stuff casing by hand, slip open end of casing over tube of large funnel and work casing onto tube until knotted end is about 1 inch from mouth of tube. Press meat mixture through funnel into casing, filling loosely. As casings are filled, twist and tie off sausage in 5-inch links. If air pockets develop in sausage, pierce casing with needle.

If sausage is not cooked immediately, wrap and refrigerate. Use within 2 days. Uncooked sausage may be frozen.

To fry bratwurst, pierce in several places with point of sharp knife, place in large saucepan and add water to cover. Heat to simmering over medium-low heat and simmer until cooked through, about 10 minutes.

Drain. Fry bratwurst in butter in large skillet over medium-low heat, turning frequently, until golden on all sides, 10 to 15 minutes.

To broil or grill bratwurst, precook as directed above and drain. Brush with melted butter and broil 3 to 4 inches from heat or grill over hot coals, turning frequently, until golden on all sides, about 10 minutes.

NOTE: To fill casing with food grinder or mixer, follow manufacturer's instructions.

SPÄTZLE

Small Egg Dumplings
6 SERVINGS

3	*cups all-purpose flour*
1	*teaspoon salt*
¼	*teaspoon ground nutmeg*
4	*eggs*
1	*cup milk*
1	*tablespoon vegetable oil*
8	*tablespoons butter*
½	*cup fine dry bread crumbs*

Stir together flour, ½ teaspoon of the salt and nutmeg in large bowl. Beat together eggs and ½ cup of the milk in medium bowl, then stir into flour mixture. Gradually stir remaining milk into flour mixture to form soft, smooth dough.

Heat 2 quarts water, oil and remaining salt to boiling in 4- or 5-quart saucepan. Force dough through holes of colander, spätzle maker or large slotted spoon with back of wooden spoon into boiling water. (If dough is too stiff to pass through holes, stir in 1 to 2 tablespoons water as needed.) Cook spätzle just until they rise to surface of boiling water, about 2 to 3 minutes. Remove with slotted spoon and drain in colander. Transfer cooked spätzle to heated serving bowl and cover to keep hot.

Cook bread crumbs in butter in large skillet over medium-high heat, stirring constantly, just until golden, about 3 minutes. Spoon over spätzle. Serve hot.

STOLLEN

German Christmas Bread

2 LOAVES

½ cup golden raisins
½ cup currants
½ cup diced citron
½ cup chopped candied or glacé cherries
2 tablespoons rum or brandy
4½ cups all-purpose flour, plus additional
    ½ cup as needed
2 packages (¼ ounce each) active dry
    yeast (2 scant tablespoons)
⅓ cup sugar
1½ teaspoons salt
½ cup milk
4 tablespoons butter, cut up
1 teaspoon grated lemon rind
2 eggs
½ teaspoon almond extract
½ cup (2 ounces) slivered blanched
    almonds
    Butter, softened
    Powdered sugar

Combine raisins, currants, citron, cherries and rum in medium bowl and let stand 1 hour.

Stir together 2 cups of the flour, yeast, sugar and salt in large bowl. Heat milk, ½ cup water, butter and lemon rind in small saucepan over low heat just until warm (115° to 120°F.). Add to flour mixture along with eggs and almond extract. Beat at low speed of electric mixer until flour is moistened. Beat at medium speed 3 minutes.

Stir ½ cup flour into fruit mixture. Stir fruit mixture, almonds and enough remaining flour into batter to make moderately stiff dough.

Turn dough onto lightly floured surface and knead until smooth and elastic, about 5 to 8 minutes. Shape into ball and place in greased bowl, turning to grease top. Cover and let rise in warm place (80° to 85°F.) until doubled in bulk, about 1 hour.

Punch dough down, cover and let rest 10 minutes. Turn out onto lightly floured surface and divide in half. Pat or roll each half into 14 × 8-inch oval and spread lightly with softened butter. Fold dough in half lengthwise, bringing upper half not quite to edge of lower half, and press firmly along edge to secure. Place loaves on lightly greased 15 × 10-inch baking sheet. Cover and let rise in warm place until doubled in bulk, about 30 minutes.

Uncover. Bake in preheated 350°F. oven until loaves are golden and sound hollow when lightly tapped, 25 to 30 minutes. Transfer to wire racks and cool completely. Sprinkle with powdered sugar.

WIENER SCHNITZEL

Veal Cutlets

6 SERVINGS

6 veal cutlets (5 to 6 ounces each),
      pounded thin
1 tablespoon fresh lemon juice
    Salt
    Freshly ground black pepper
½ cup all-purpose flour
2 eggs
1 cup fine dry bread crumbs
3 to 5 tablespoons butter
3 tablespoons vegetable oil

FOR GARNISH:

6 thin slices lemon
6 rolled anchovies
1 tablespoon drained capers

Sprinkle cutlets with lemon juice and let stand 30 minutes. Pat dry with paper towels and sprinkle one side of each cutlet lightly with salt and pepper. Dip cutlets into flour to coat both sides evenly, shaking to remove excess flour. In shallow bowl or pie plate, beat eggs and 2 tablespoons cold water together with fork until frothy. Place bread crumbs in similar bowl. Dip cutlets into egg mixture to coat both sides evenly, then dip into crumbs to coat both sides evenly. Place on waxed paper or plate.

Sauté breaded cutlets, 2 or 3 at a time, in 3 tablespoons butter and the oil in large skillet over medium heat. Cook until golden, 4 to 6 minutes on each side. Transfer to heated serving platter and keep warm in preheated 225°F. oven while cooking remaining cutlets. Add remaining butter to skillet as necessary. Before serving, garnish each cutlet with lemon slice, anchovy and a few capers.

SCHWARZWALDER KIRSCHTORTE

Black Forest Cherry Cake
12 SERVINGS

½ pound fresh dark sweet cherries, pitted
     or 1 cup canned dark sweet cherries,
     drained and pitted
8 tablespoons Kirschwasser
½ cup sifted cake flour
½ cup sifted cocoa
6 eggs, separated
1½ cups granulated sugar
1 teaspoon vanilla extract
½ teaspoon salt
½ teaspoon cream of tartar
5 tablespoons butter, clarified (see Note)
     Cocoa and butter (for pan)
2 cups heavy cream
½ cup powdered sugar
     Semisweet chocolate curls

Combine cherries and 2 tablespoons of the Kirschwasser in small saucepan and let stand while preparing cake.

Sift together flour and cocoa. Beat egg yolks in small bowl with electric mixer on high speed until very thick and lemon-colored, about 5 minutes. Add ½ cup of the granulated sugar, vanilla and salt. Beat until sugar is dissolved and mixture forms a ribbon when beater is lifted, 2 to 3 minutes.

Wash and dry beaters thoroughly. Beat egg whites and cream of tartar in large mixer bowl at high speed until foamy, then gradually beat in ½ cup granulated sugar. Beat until stiff peaks form and sugar is dissolved.

Gently fold dry mixture into yolk mixture. Fold 2 large spoonfuls of egg whites into yolk mixture. Pour yolk mixture over remaining whites and gently fold together just until blended. Gently fold in butter, about 2 tablespoons at a time. Divide batter evenly between 2 buttered and co-coa-dusted 8-inch round cake pans. Bake in preheated 350°F. oven until center of cake springs back when lightly touched, 25 to 30 minutes. Cool cakes 5 minutes, carefully re-move from pans and cool on wire racks.

Add 2 tablespoons water to cherries in saucepan. Heat to simmering over medium-low heat. Reduce heat to low and simmer until cherries are tender, about 5 minutes. Drain, re-serving liquid. Heat 2 tablespoons of the liquid and remaining ½ cup gran-ulated sugar to simmering in small saucepan over medium-low heat. Simmer until very syrupy, about 3 minutes. Remove from heat and stir in 4 tablespoons Kirschwasser.

Cut cake layers in half horizontally to make 4 thin layers. Drizzle syrup mixture evenly over cut sides of each layer, spreading with spatula to cover evenly.

Fresh, sweet cherries, heavy cream and Kirschwasser add richness to the celebrated Schwarzwalder Kirschetorte.

Black Forest Cherry Cake *is served on an elegant Bavarian cake platter, accompanied by a glass of White Riesling.*

Whip cream in medium bowl at high speed until soft peaks form, then add powdered sugar and remaining 2 tablespoons Kirschwasser. Continue beating until stiff peaks are formed.

Place 1 cake layer, cut side up, on serving plate. Spread with scant ¾ cup whipped cream. Top with second cake layer, cut side down; spread with scant ¾ cup whipped cream. Reserve 6 cherries for garnish and arrange remaining cherries over whipped cream on cake layers. Top with third cake layer, cut side up, and spread with scant ¾ cup whipped cream. Top with final cake layer, cut side down. Frost top and sides of cake with remaining whipped cream. Garnish with reserved cherries and chocolate curls. Refrigerate until serving time. Cut into wedges to serve.

NOTE: To clarify butter, heat in small saucepan over low heat until melted but not browned. Remove pan from heat and let stand 1 minute. Spoon off and discard any foam from top. Tilt pan slightly and spoon clear butter into small bowl, discarding milky solids.

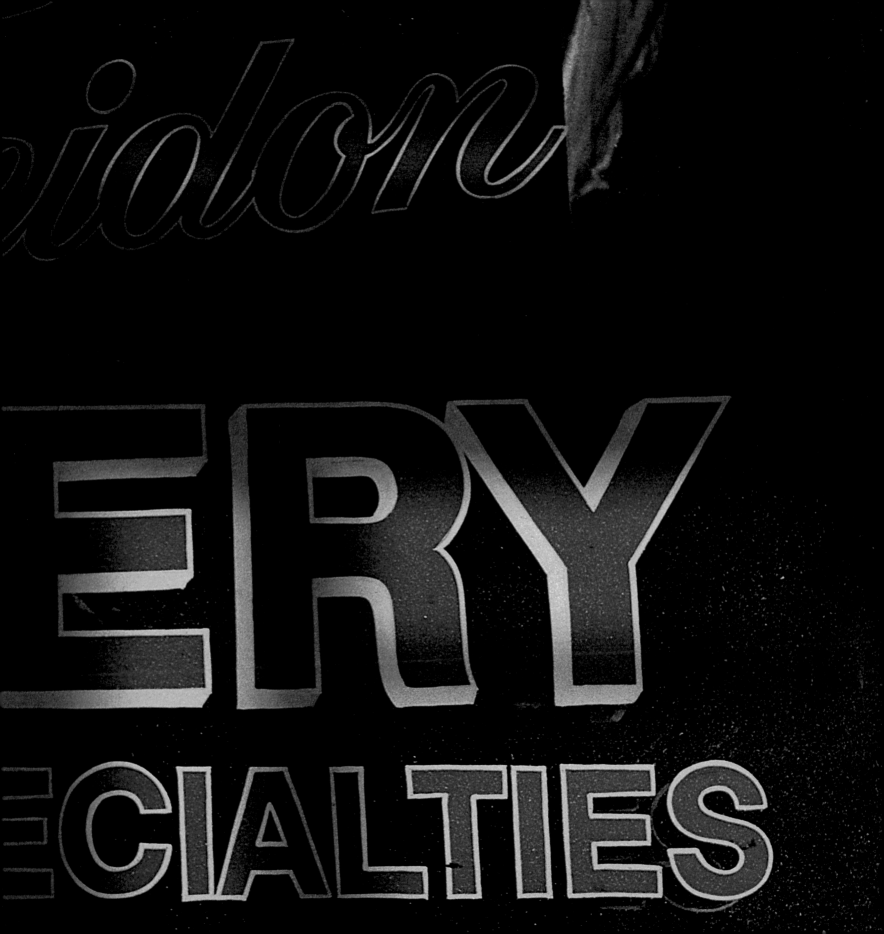

Greece

Traditional Greek Dinner Menu

Taramosaláta (Carp Roe Dip)
Saganaki (Fried Cheese)
Soúpa Avgolémono (Egg-Lemon Soup)
Psari Plaki (Baked Fish)
Dolmáthes (Stuffed Grape Leaves)
Arni Souvlaki (Lamb Kabobs)
Pilaf
Baklava (Greek Pastry)
Coffee

RECOMMENDED WINES

Semillon Blanc
Merlot
Muscat Canelli

Additional Recipes

Moussaka (Eggplant and Meat Casserole)
Stifado (Beef Stew with Onions and Cheese)
Punjene Paprika (Stuffed Green Peppers)
Tarator (Yogurt and Cucumber Soup)
Salata Horiatika (Peasant Salad)
Vegetables à la Grecque (Greek-Style Mixed Vegetables)
Vasilopeta (Greek New Year's Bread)
Lambropsomo (Greek Easter Bread)

A boatload of some of the 40,000 Greek-Americans who returned to Greece to fight in the 1912–1913 Balkan wars. Many of them would enlist again in the American Expeditionary Forces in World War I.

Greeks and Americans have always had an irresistible bond. The American government is founded on ancient Greek democratic ideals and a belief in tolerance, even reverence, for the expression of personal opinion. It has been said that if two Greeks talk, three ideas emerge; if four Greek soldiers meet, five generals spring into being. When Greece faced an economic crisis in the 1890s and needed a second arena in which to better her finances, her people almost inevitably headed for the sympathetic environment of America.

The Greek crisis was triggered by agricultural disaster in France. In 1863, French vineyards lost a major war with insects and began buying currants from Greece. The Greeks obligingly stepped up currant production, even destroying their slow-growing olive orchards to do so. When the Gallic vineyards recovered, France promptly banned Greek imports. Greek farmers were left with 70,000 tons of unsalable fruit and a new incentive to try their luck elsewhere.

Yet another motive, much nearer the heart, spurred the Greek exodus: the desire to restore a Panhellenic nation. Partially freed from Turkish rule in 1829, Greece burned to unite her "unredeemed" compatriots in Macedonia, Crete and the Aegean Islands. As a result, unlike many who came through Ellis Island, Greek immigrants were not just seeking a better life for themselves. They were die-hard patriots who intended to strengthen Greece with American earnings.

They brought their own brand of hardy ingenuity. One newly arrived group, abandoned in Canada when promised work evaporated after a week, found its way back to the United States through deep, wild forests without food, maps or guides and eventually settled in Boston. Other immigrants' stories resembled that of Demetrios Paleologas. As a teenager in Greece, he took an undersized horse his father had bought for 275 drachmas and sold it, after it fell ill, for 300. "This boy, my son, he's going to succeed!" the elder Paleologas announced. "I'm going to send him to America." He did, and Demetrios became a millionaire restaurateur.

Opening restaurants, shoeshine parlors and fruit, flower and candy stores, Greek farmers applied their versatility and native business acumen to become luxury-service entrepreneurs in urban America. Some Greeks hammered home railroad ties in the West and some fished for sponges near the heavily Greek city of Tarpon Springs, Florida, but most entered the uncharted territory of the business world. "No one knows why so many Greeks became prominent as restaurant owners or cooks," according to the *Harvard Encyclopedia of American Ethnic Groups*. But Vilma Chantiles, author of *The Foods of Greece*, offers a hint when she quotes the poet Menander (third century B.C.): "Not a single person has ever escaped scot-free after he wronged a cook. Our profession is somehow sacrosanct."

While shining shoes was not a sacrosanct task in Greece, many young boys, wooed by the Greek *padrone* system, spent their first couple of years in America literally gaining a toehold on prosperity by working seventeen hours a day in shoeshine parlors. Starting a business on the street was no easier. As one aspiring confectioner wrote: "All day we sell candy with a basket tied around our neck, and they call us in American, English, German, dago, that is, beggars, and so many names we do not understand. If we did understand we would be going to jail every day."

Greeks may have struggled with a foreign language, but their literacy rate was high. Nationalism and the Greek Orthodox

Church, two inseparable ruling forces, required that male citizens have some knowledge of history and religion. The Greek passion for politics ensured a commensurate obsession with newspapers. Greek publications flourished in America, with readers on guard against any slippage in the purity of the language. Thomas Burgess, author of *The Greeks in America*, observed: "The bellboy who respectfully carries up the grip of some great American millionaire pork packer is in all likelihood the much more cultured man of the two."

That same bellboy probably fed his hunger for home at a *kaffeneion*, or coffeehouse. The all-male *kaffeneion*, invented in 1652 by a Cretan, offered thick, sweet Greek coffee, honey- and nut-laden baklava, card games, music, dancing, billows of tobacco smoke and the crucial ingredient: talk. Lively discussion of everything, but especially Greek politics, nourished the spirit more than roasted lamb or retsina could.

The *kaffeneions'* importance diminished slightly with the arrival of Greek women. Horrified by the free ways of American women, Greek men either went home to marry or imported a bride vouched for by relatives and friends. Greek Orthodox wedding ceremonies were noted for their solemn beauty, the wedding receptions for their vitality. Amid the dancing and celebration, guests rewarded musicians by wetting one- and five-dollar bills with their tongues and pasting them on each player's forehead.

An inimitable gusto brightened all Greek Orthodox holidays and festivals, which became more important in America as tangible links to God and to Greece. Easter outshone the rest. Greeks observed the forty-day Lenten fast and then, after singing the Resurrection Song at midnight Mass, shot skyrockets and firecrackers. Families returned home to a ceremonial breakfast fea-

The immigrant spirit meets the challenges of a new land.

turing *mayeritsa*, a stew of kidneys, liver and the intestines of the paschal lamb, seasoned with butter and thyme and covered with an egg and lemon sauce. Salads, breads, cakes, sweets and white wine were also served. Before eating, each person cracked a red-dyed egg, symbolizing the blood of Christ, against his neighbor's egg. The sturdier the shell, the greater its owner's good fortune in the coming year.

No one can say how many Greek Americans hoped good fortune would include a permanent return to Greece. By 1907 fully one-fourth of the country's work force had emigrated, causing considerable dismay at home. Greek newspapers, trying to halt the flow, printed letters from disenchanted immigrants, predicting illness and even death. The American financial panic of 1907 briefly answered Greek prayers. Then the phenomenal optimism of the immigrant, bolstered by the Greek love of adventure, reopened the floodgates. One Cretan merchant cheerfully capitalized on the nation's anxiety by selling American fertilizer. "Instead of going to the United States, we bring the United States to Crete," he explained.

That was precisely the original intent of most Greek immigrants. They planned to establish themselves and pay any debts, support their families in Greece, raise dowries for all unmarried sisters and save some money. Finally they would return wealthy and triumphant, marry a good Greek girl and contribute to the glory of Greece.

Many managed the visit home. But most confirmed Greek fears by settling permanently in the United States. Greek-Americans became a people devoted to two nations. They adopted America with loyalty and generosity and were quick to volunteer for American military action, but they still stood by their Greek roots with unshakable patriotism. They developed Greek-language schools for their American-born children and poured so many American dollars into the Greek economy that Greece became dependent and could not pass laws barring emigration.

In 1912–1913, at the onset of the Balkan Wars, more than 40,000 Greek-Americans sailed home to fight the Turks. After a victorious tour of duty, the majority gathered up their relatives for the journey to America. An Athenian, watching this use of Greek resources, asked the question still preoccupying many Greeks: "In the end, does emigration benefit or harm?" His conclusion rang with Greek magnanimity. "When we see the emigrants returning courageous, robust, disciplined, so healthy that when they walk the surface beneath them cracks, we believe that emigration benefits."

Greek-American volunteers prepare to leave New York to fight in the Balkan wars.

TARATOR

Yogurt and Cucumber Soup
6 SERVINGS

¾   cup coarsely chopped walnuts
4   large cloves garlic, halved
3   tablespoons olive oil
4   cups (2 pints) plain yogurt
3   medium cucumbers, pared and seeded
½   teaspoon salt
⅛   teaspoon freshly ground black pepper
1   tablespoon chopped fresh mint

Place walnuts and garlic in blender container and blend until coarsely ground. Add oil and blend until smooth. Gradually blend in yogurt, scraping down sides of container frequently with rubber spatula. Pour into glass bowl.

Shred cucumbers. Place in colander or sieve and press out excess liquid. Stir cucumbers, salt and pepper into yogurt mixture. Cover with plastic wrap and refrigerate until thoroughly chilled, at least 2 hours. Spoon into individual bowls. Garnish each serving with about ½ teaspoon chopped mint.

SOÚPA AVGOLÉMONO

Egg-Lemon Soup
6 SERVINGS

6   cups rich homemade chicken broth
⅓   cup long-grain rice
3   eggs
⅓   cup fresh lemon juice
1½   tablespoons chopped fresh dill or
        parsley
¼   teaspoon salt
      Pinch freshly ground white pepper

FOR GARNISH:

6   lemon slices

Bring broth to boil in 2-quart saucepan over high heat. Stir in rice. Reduce heat to low, cover and simmer until rice is cooked, about 25 minutes.

Beat eggs in medium bowl until thick, about 2 minutes. Beat in lemon juice. Gradually blend in about 1 cup hot broth. Slowly blend egg mixture into broth in saucepan. Cook, stirring constantly, until soup is smooth and thick but not boiling, 1 to 2 minutes. Remove from heat. Stir in dill, salt and pepper. Serve immediately, garnishing each serving with lemon slice.

SAGANÁKI

Fried Cheese
4 TO 6 SERVINGS

½ pound Kasseri cheese
½ cup all-purpose flour
6 tablespoons butter
2 tablespoons fresh lemon juice
1½ tablespoons cognac or brandy

Cut cheese horizontally into 3 equal slices, each ¼ to ½ inch thick. Immerse in ice water in medium bowl in refrigerator at least 1 hour before frying.

Drain one slice and pat dry with paper towels. Dip in flour to coat evenly, shaking off excess. Heat 2 tablespoons butter in small skillet over medium-high heat until sizzling. Add cheese and fry quickly just until lightly browned, about 1 minute on each side. Remove skillet from heat. Sprinkle cheese with 2 teaspoons lemon juice and 1½ teaspoons cognac. Ignite with long wooden match. Serve when flame is extinguished. Repeat process with remaining cheese, serving immediately.

PSARI PLAKI

Baked Fish
4 TO 6 SERVINGS

1 whole red snapper (2½ to 3 pounds), dressed, or 2 pounds fresh fish fillets or steaks (bass, red snapper, codfish or halibut)
4 tablespoons olive oil
½ cup dry white wine
1 tablespoon fresh lemon juice
½ cup chopped onion
1 clove garlic, minced
½ cup tomato sauce
3 tablespoons finely chopped fresh parsley
½ teaspoon dried oregano, crumbled
2 medium ripe tomatoes, sliced ¼ inch thick
1 lemon, thinly sliced
¼ cup fine dry bread crumbs
2 tablespoons thinly sliced green onions, including tops

Rinse fish under cold running water. Pat dry with paper towels. Brush 1 tablespoon oil over bottom of large baking dish. Pour in wine. Add fish and sprinkle with lemon juice.

Sauté onion and garlic in 2 tablespoons oil in small saucepan over medium heat until onion is soft, about 5 minutes. Stir in tomato sauce, 1 tablespoon parsley and oregano. Simmer, uncovered, 5 minutes. Spoon mixture over fish.

Arrange tomato and lemon slices over fish. Combine bread crumbs and remaining oil and stir in green onions and remaining parsley. Sprinkle over tomato and lemon slices.

Bake in preheated 350°F. oven until fish flakes easily when tested with fork at thickest part, 25 to 30 minutes. Serve immediately.

DOLMÁTHES

Stuffed Grape Leaves
3½ TO 4 DOZEN

3/4 pound ground lamb
3/4 cup finely chopped onion
1 clove garlic, finely chopped
2 tablespoons olive oil
1/3 cup long-grain rice
2 tablespoons minced fresh parsley
1 teaspoon finely chopped fresh mint (1/2 teaspoon dried)
1/2 teaspoon salt
1/8 teaspoon freshly ground black pepper
1 jar (8 or 9 ounces) grape leaves, drained
1 1/2 cups rich homemade beef broth
2 tablespoons butter, melted

FOR GARNISH:

Lemon wedges

Cook lamb, onion and garlic in oil in large skillet over medium-high heat (breaking up meat with fork) until onion is soft, about 10 minutes. Stir in rice and seasonings. Cook, stirring constantly, until rice is coated with oil, about 2 minutes. Add ¾ cup water. Reduce heat to low. Cover and simmer until rice has absorbed all liquid, about 20 minutes.

Bring 2 quarts water to boil in 5-quart Dutch oven over high heat. Add grape leaves and immediately remove from heat. Let stand 1 minute. Transfer leaves to colander and quickly cool with cold running water. Separate leaves and lay out on paper towels, dull sides up. Pat dry.

Place 1 level tablespoonful meat and rice mixture in center of each leaf. Fold edges of leaf over to cover filling completely. Roll up.

Arrange filled leaves, folded edges down, in greased 5-quart Dutch oven. Pour broth over leaves and drizzle with melted butter. Place heatproof plate on top to prevent rolls from unfolding. Cover and simmer over low heat until tender, 25 to 30 minutes. Drain. Serve hot, garnished with lemon wedges.

RIGHT: Grape leaves await a filling of lamb, chopped onion, olive oil and herbs in this presentation of Dolmáthes.
OVERLEAF: Onions, garlic, mushrooms and green peppers complement juicy pieces of lamb in Arni Souvláki.

ARNI SOUVLÁKI

Lamb Kabobs
6 SERVINGS

¼	cup dry red wine
¼	cup olive oil
3	tablespoons fresh lemon juice
1	small onion, grated
2	cloves garlic, minced
1	teaspoon salt
1	teaspoon dried oregano, crumbled
⅛	teaspoon dried thyme, crumbled
⅛	teaspoon freshly ground black pepper
2	pounds boneless leg of lamb, cut into 1½-inch cubes
12	large mushroom caps, cleaned
2	green peppers, cored, seeded and cut into 1½-inch dice
1	medium onion, peeled and cut into 6 wedges

TO SERVE:

Pilaf (recipe follows)

Combine wine, oil, lemon juice, grated onion, garlic, salt, oregano, thyme and pepper in large glass bowl. Add lamb and toss to coat completely. Cover and refrigerate at least 3 hours, turning lamb occasionally.

Drain lamb, reserving marinade. Thread lamb cubes onto skewers, alternating with vegetables and leaving small space between each ingredient. Brush vegetables with marinade.

Broil 4 to 5 inches from heat or grill over charcoal outdoors, turning skewers and basting frequently, until lamb is done, 10 to 15 minutes. Serve hot with *Pilaf.*

PILAF

6 SERVINGS

⅓	cup finely chopped onion
4	tablespoons butter
1½	cups long-grain rice
3	cups rich homemade chicken broth
½	teaspoon salt
⅛	teaspoon freshly ground black pepper

Sauté onion in 2 tablespoons butter in medium saucepan over medium heat until soft but not browned, about 5 minutes. Stir in rice. Cook, stirring constantly, until rice is completely coated with butter, about 2 minutes. Add broth, salt and pepper. Reduce heat to low, cover and cook until all liquid is absorbed, about 20 minutes.

Stir remaining butter into rice. Remove from heat and let stand 10 minutes before serving.

BAKLAVA

Greek Pastry

3 DOZEN

1¼ *cups sugar*
1   *teaspoon ground cinnamon*
⅛   *teaspoon ground cloves*
2   *cups finely chopped or ground walnuts*
2   *cups finely chopped or ground blanched almonds*
1   *pound prepared phyllo dough*
20   *tablespoons butter, melted*
2   *tablespoons fresh lemon juice*
6   *whole cloves*
1   *stick cinnamon*
1   *cup honey*

Blend ½ cup sugar, cinnamon and cloves in medium bowl. Stir in nuts.

Carefully unfold phyllo sheets and cover with damp towel. Place 1 sheet phyllo over bottom of greased 13 × 9 × 2-inch baking dish, folding edges over to fit dish. Brush lightly with melted butter. Top with 3 more sheets of phyllo, folding each to fit pan and buttering each. Sprinkle with about ½ cup nut mixture. Top with 2 more sheets phyllo, buttering each while layering. Sprinkle with ⅓ cup nut mixture. Continue layering 2 sheets phyllo and ⅓ cup nut mixture until all ingredients are used, ending with phyllo.

With sharp knife, carefully cut diamond shapes in top of baklava: Make parallel, diagonal cuts about 1½ inches apart and ½ inch deep, then cross with parallel, diagonal cuts in opposite direction. Bake in preheated 350°F. oven until golden, about 1 hour.

Combine remaining sugar, ¾ cup water, lemon juice, whole cloves and cinnamon stick in medium saucepan. Bring to boil over medium-high heat. Reduce heat to low and cook 15 minutes. Stir in honey and continue cooking just until mixture boils. Remove from heat and cool to room temperature. Strain.

When baklava is cooked, transfer to wire rack. Immediately pour cooled honey mixture evenly over. Cool to room temperature. Using sharp knife, cut out diamond shapes along scored lines, cutting completely through all layers.

MOUSSAKÁ

Eggplant and Meat Casserole

6 TO 8 SERVINGS

2 medium eggplants (about 1½ pounds
   each), pared and sliced ½ inch thick
   Salt
1 medium onion, peeled and finely
   chopped
1 cup olive oil
1½ pounds lean ground lamb or beef or
   combination of both
2 medium ripe tomatoes, peeled, seeded
   and finely chopped
½ cup dry white wine
¼ cup tomato paste
2 tablespoons finely chopped fresh parsley
1 clove garlic, minced
1 teaspoon salt
½ teaspoon dried oregano, crumbled
¼ teaspoon ground cinnamon
⅛ teaspoon ground allspice
⅛ teaspoon freshly ground black pepper
¼ cup fine dry bread crumbs
½ cup all-purpose flour
1 cup grated Kasseri or Parmesan cheese
   Yogurt Sauce (recipe follows)

Place eggplant slices in colander and sprinkle lightly with salt. Cover with heavy plate and drain 30 minutes.

Saute onion in 2 tablespoons oil in large skillet over medium heat until soft, about 5 minutes. Add meat. Cook until meat is browned, 8 to 10 minutes, breaking meat up with fork. Stir in tomatoes, wine, tomato paste, parsley, garlic and seasonings. Continue cooking, stirring frequently, until most liquid has evaporated, about 10 minutes. Remove from heat and stir in bread crumbs.

Pat eggplant slices dry with paper towels. Dip in flour to coat both sides evenly, shaking off excess flour. Sauté eggplant in remaining oil in large skillet over medium heat until lightly browned, about 2 minutes on each side.

Arrange half the slices in greased 13x9x2-inch baking dish. Sprinkle with ⅓ cup grated cheese. Spread meat evenly over eggplant and sprinkle with ⅓ cup cheese. Top with remaining eggplant.

Pour *Yogurt Sauce* evenly over eggplant. Sprinkle with remaining cheese. Bake in preheated 375°F. oven until top is golden and puffed,

40 to 45 minutes. Remove from oven and let stand 10 minutes. To serve, cut into squares.

YOGURT SAUCE

3 eggs
1 tablespoon all-purpose flour
2 cups (1 pint) plain yogurt
1/2 teaspoon salt
1/8 teaspoon freshly ground white pepper
1/8 teaspoon ground nutmeg

Beat eggs with whisk in 1½-quart saucepan. Blend in flour and yogurt. Add seasonings. Cook over medium-low heat, stirring frequently, until mixture comes to a boil and thickens, 6 to 8 minutes.

STIFADO

Beef Stew with Onions and Cheese
6 SERVINGS

3 pounds lean boneless beef round or chuck, cut into 2-inch cubes
4 tablespoons butter
1/4 cup olive oil
1½ cups dry red wine
3/4 cup tomato paste
3 cloves garlic, minced
3 tablespoons red wine vinegar
2 large bay leaves
1 cinnamon stick, halved
1 teaspoon salt
1/4 teaspoon freshly ground black pepper
1 pound small white onions
1 cup crumbled feta cheese

Cook beef, about 1 pound at a time, in butter and oil in 5-quart Dutch oven over medium-high heat. Stir frequently until evenly browned, 8 to 10 minutes.

Drain fat from pan. Add 1½ cups water, wine, tomato paste, garlic, vinegar, bay leaves, cinnamon, salt and pepper. Bring to boil over medium-high heat, stirring occasionally. Reduce heat to low. Cover and cook, stirring occasionally, until beef is almost tender, about 1¼ hours.

Bring remaining 2½ cups water to boil over high heat in medium saucepan. Add onions and cook 2 minutes. Transfer to colander, cool with cold running water and peel. Stir onions into beef mixture. Cover and continue cooking until beef and onions are tender, about 15 minutes longer.

Discard cinnamon stick and bay leaves. Stir in cheese. Cook, uncovered, until cheese softens, about 2 minutes. Serve hot.

PUNJENE PAPRIKA

Stuffed Green Peppers
6 SERVINGS

6   large green peppers
¼   cup long-grain rice
1   small onion, peeled and chopped
2   tablespoons vegetable oil
½   pound lean ground pork
½   pound lean ground beef
1   tablespoon finely chopped fresh parsley
½   teaspoon salt
1¼   teaspoons sweet paprika
⅛   teaspoon freshly ground black pepper
2   medium tomatoes, peeled, seeded and chopped
1   cup rich homemade beef broth
¼   cup dairy sour cream

Cut thin slice from stem end of each pepper. Discard seeds and thick white membranes. Rinse peppers. If necessary, cut thin slice from bottom of each to prevent tipping.

Bring ½ cup water to boil in small saucepan over high heat. Stir in rice. Reduce heat to low and simmer 5 minutes. Drain.

Sauté onion in oil in large skillet over medium heat until soft, about 5 minutes. Add pork and beef and cook, breaking up meat with fork until lightly browned, 8 to 10 minutes. Spoon off excess fat. Stir in rice, parsley, salt, ¼ teaspoon paprika and pepper.

Distribute tomatoes evenly over bottom of lightly greased 5-quart Dutch oven. Spoon about ½ cup meat mixture into each green pepper. Place peppers over tomatoes. Combine broth and remaining paprika and pour around peppers. Cover and cook over low heat until peppers are tender, about 45 minutes.

Transfer peppers to heated serving dish, cover and keep warm. Pour pan liquid into a blender container or food processor fitted with metal blade. Blend or process until smooth, about 10 seconds. Return liquid to Dutch oven and cook over high heat until reduced to 1 cup, about 5 minutes. Remove from heat. Stir in sour cream and pour mixture over peppers. Serve immediately.

Punjene Paprika, *fresh from the oven, are garnished with sour cream before serving.*

TARAMOSALÁTA

Carp Roe Dip

2 CUPS

5 slices white bread, crusts removed
½ cup (¼ pound) tarama (carp roe) or red caviar
¼ cup fresh lemon juice
¼ cup finely chopped green onions
¾ cup olive oil

TO SERVE:

Minced fresh parsley
Greek black olives
Crackers, toasted bread rounds and/or raw vegetables

Place bread in medium bowl and add water to cover. Let stand 5 minutes. Squeeze dry.

Place bread, tarama, lemon juice and onions in blender container. Blend until smooth, stopping motor frequently to scrape down sides. With motor running, gradually add oil in thin steady stream. Stop motor when all oil is added.

Pour dip into serving bowl and sprinkle with parsley. Arrange olives around edge of bowl. Serve with crackers, bread or vegetables.

VASILOPETA

Greek New Year's Bread

1 LARGE LOAF

8 tablespoons sugar
1 package active dry yeast (1 scant tablespoon)
½ cup milk
4 tablespoons butter
1 tablespoon grated orange rind
1 teaspoon salt
½ teaspoon ground cinnamon
¼ teaspoon ground nutmeg
3 eggs, slightly beaten
4 cups all-purpose flour, plus additional ¼ cup as needed
Vegetable oil

Combine ¼ cup warm (110° to 115°F.) water, 1 tablespoon sugar and yeast. Stir to dissolve yeast. Let stand until bubbly, about 5 minutes.

Heat remaining sugar, milk, butter, orange rind, salt, cinnamon and nutmeg in small saucepan over low heat just until warm. Pour into large mixing bowl. Measure 2 tablespoons beaten eggs into small bowl, cover with plastic wrap and reserve. Beat remaining eggs and yeast mixture into milk mixture. Beat in 1½ cups flour until smooth, about 2 minutes on medium speed of electric mixer or 300 strokes by hand. Stir in additional flour to make moderately stiff dough.

Turn dough onto lightly floured surface. Knead until smooth and sat-

Garnished with freshly chopped parsley, Taramosaláta features red caviar.

iny, 8 to 10 minutes. Shape dough into ball and place in lightly greased bowl, turning to grease all sides. Cover and let rise in warm place until doubled in bulk, about 1½ hours.

Punch dough down, cover and let rest 10 minutes. Shape dough into ball and place on large greased baking sheet. Roll or pat into circle 6 inches in diameter. Brush lightly with oil. Let stand in warm place until almost doubled in bulk, 30 to 40 minutes.

Brush loaf with reserved egg. Bake in preheated 350°F. oven until golden brown, 30 to 35 minutes. Transfer to wire rack and cool completely.

SALATA HORIATIKI

Peasant Salad
6 SERVINGS

1 large head romaine lettuce, washed, drained and chilled
2 medium tomatoes, cut into ½-inch wedges
1 large cucumber, cleaned and sliced ⅛-inch thick
6 to 8 radishes, trimmed and thinly sliced
4 green onions, cut into ¼-inch slices
6 ounces feta cheese, coarsely crumbled
¼ pound imported Greek black olives
1 teaspoon finely chopped fresh mint
½ cup olive oil
3 tablespoons fresh lemon juice
2 tablespoons red wine vinegar
1 clove garlic, crushed
½ teaspoon finely chopped fresh oregano

Tear lettuce into bite-sized pieces, discarding any tough stem ends or discolored leaves. Place in large salad bowl. Add tomatoes, cucumber, radishes, green onions, cheese and olives. Sprinkle with mint. Blend all remaining ingredients in small bowl with whisk. Pour over salad and toss lightly until thoroughly mixed. Serve immediately.

LAMBROPSOMO

Greek Easter Bread
1 LARGE LOAF

4¾ cups all-purpose flour, plus additional ½ cup as needed
2 packages active dry yeast (2 scant tablespoons)
½ teaspoon ground allspice
½ cup milk
½ cup sugar
4 tablespoons butter
1½ teaspoons anise seeds
1 teaspoon salt
4 eggs
  Vegetable oil

Large chunks of feta cheese and Greek olives top Salata Horiatiki, *served on a platter from Skyros, circa 1910.*

5   hard-cooked, unshelled eggs, dyed red
3   tablespoons sesame seeds

Stir together 2 cups flour, yeast and allspice in large mixing bowl. Heat milk, ½ cup water, sugar, butter, anise seeds and salt in small saucepan over low heat just until warm (115° to 120°F.). Add to flour mixture. Beat until smooth, about 2 minutes on medium speed of electric mixer or 300 strokes by hand.

Separate white from one egg and place in small bowl. Cover with plastic wrap. Beat remaining eggs and yolk into flour mixture. Add 1 cup flour. Beat 1 minute on medium speed or 150 strokes by hand. Stir in additional flour to make moderately stiff dough.

Turn dough onto lightly floured surface. Knead until smooth and satiny, 10 to 12 minutes. Shape dough into ball and place in lightly greased bowl, turning to grease all sides. Cover and let rise in warm place until doubled in bulk, about 1½ hours.

Punch dough down. Cover and let rest 10 minutes. Reserve about ⅙ of dough. Shape remainder into smooth ball and place on large greased baking sheet. Roll or pat into circle 9 inches in diameter. Place 1 dyed egg on center of dough, pressing slightly to push partially into dough. Place remaining 4 dyed eggs near edges of dough to form tips of a cross.

Divide reserved dough into 10 equal pieces. Roll each between palms and work surface to make a 6-inch rope. Place two ropes crosswise over each egg. Pinch ends of ropes into dough to secure eggs. Brush loaf with oil. Cover and let stand in warm place until doubled in bulk, about 1 hour.

Beat reserved egg white with fork until frothy. Brush over loaf. Sprinkle with sesame seeds. Bake in preheated 350°F. oven until top is evenly browned and dough sounds hollow in center when tapped, 40 to 45 minutes. Transfer to wire rack and cool.

VEGETABLES À LA GRECQUE

Greek-Style Mixed Vegetables

6 SERVINGS

3   large carrots, pared
2   large leeks, cleaned
1   small eggplant (about 1 pound)
2   medium zucchini
¼   to ½ pound fresh mushrooms, cleaned
⅓   cup dry white wine
2   tablespoons fresh lemon juice

2   tablespoons olive oil
4   shallots or 2 green onions, chopped
½   teaspoon salt
¼   teaspoon dried thyme, crumbled
⅛   teaspoon freshly ground black pepper
2   tablespoons chopped fresh parsley
2   teaspoons chopped fresh mint

Cut carrots in half crosswise, then cut in half lengthwise. Cut white part of leeks into 3-inch pieces and cut each in half lengthwise. Cut zucchini crosswise into 3-inch pieces, then cut each piece lengthwise into quarters and reserve. Cut large mushrooms in half; leave small mushrooms whole.

Combine 1 cup water, wine, lemon juice, oil, shallots, salt, thyme and pepper in 3-quart saucepan. Bring to boil over medium-high heat.

Reduce heat to low. Add carrots and leeks to simmering liquid and cook, uncovered, 5 minutes. Cut eggplant into 8 wedges, add to saucepan and cook 5 minutes. Add zucchini and mushrooms and cook until all vegetables are crisp-tender, about 5 minutes longer. Remove vegetables from saucepan with slotted spoon and transfer to heated serving bowl. Cover to keep hot.

Bring pan liquid to boil over high heat. Boil until reduced to about ½ cup, 6 to 8 minutes. Pour over vegetables. Sprinkle with parsley and mint. Serve hot.

A colorful mix of Greek-style vegetables is presented on a platter from the island of Rhodes, circa 1910.

Great Britain

Afternoon Tea Menu

Tea Sandwiches
Potted Shrimp
Chilled Celery Stalks
Crumpets
Blueberry Tea Scones
Richmond Maids of Honour
Tea

High Tea Menu

Welsh Rarebit
Celery Stalks
Carrot Sticks and Cherry Tomatoes
Crumpets
Bath Buns
Trifle
Tea

RECOMMENDED WINES

Johannisberg Riesling
Chenin Blanc
Rosé of Cabernet

Additional Recipes

Steak and Kidney Pie
Cornish Pasties
Irish Soda Bread
Yorkshire Pudding
Bubble and Squeak
Cock-a-Leekie Soup

The English are usually thought to have come to America in search of religious freedom. In truth, the very first settlers were hunting something more tangible: gold. Sir Walter Raleigh, dashing favorite of Queen Elizabeth I, organized two attempts at colonization in the 1580s "to seek new worlds for gold, for praise, for glory." One group returned home after a year; the other, which landed on Roanoke Island in 1587, had vanished without a trace when the next ship from England arrived three years later.

Their disappearance failed to discourage the gentleman adventurers who settled Jamestown, Virginia, in 1607. At Jamestown, wrote Captain John Smith in his *Generall Historie of Virginia*, there was "no talke, no hope, nor worke, but dig gold, wash gold, refine gold, load gold." During this pursuit of nonexistent riches, Smith, a man of rare practicality, forced the settlers to plant Indian corn and other crops. By 1614 Jamestown had sent its first shipment of cured tobacco to England. "Sotweed" proved such an instant, widespread success that the economic future of Virginia was assured.

Six years later, the *Mayflower* dropped anchor at Plymouth Rock. Fifty-one Separatist Puritans, popularly known as Pilgrims, and fifty "Strangers"—ordinary settlers, hired hands and indentured servants—agreed while still on board to form a "civil body Politick." The government they roughed out in the Mayflower Compact was the precursor of American democracy.

The Puritans had crossed the Atlantic for an ideal, but they were also, according to Francis Brown in *One America*, "a cantankerous lot, quarreling constantly among each other.... They were interested in making money in their new home and, from the

The faces of Irish immigrants light up with hope just before their ship docks in New York.

On shore at last, this English immigrant family poses for a picture after debarking from the S.S. Adriatic *on April 17, 1908.*

first, there appeared that hunger for land which eventually carried descendants of the settlers across the continent.''

Benevolent Indians in the North and South helped the English stave off more immediate hungers, introducing them to corn, beans, squash, pumpkins and native game and fish. But the English cast a wary eye on most wild foreign food. They clung to old eating habits when possible and hastened to import supplies from home. As a result of this culinary patriotism, many Americans still feel inexplicably comforted by chicken, pork, wheat bread, apples and sweet desserts.

The English arrived in two groups: a middle class of yeomen and merchants; and a lower class of indentured servants. Members of the middle class, more accustomed to established commerce than to stump-grubbing, were often appalled by life on the agrarian frontier. Bound laborers, arriving with a grittier perspective, played a key role in colonial survival, especially in the South. But both groups maintained a stiff upper lip and carried on. By 1690, for the first and last time, 90 percent of the American population was English.

During the seventeenth century, as the English settled from New England to Georgia, Presbyterian Lowlanders moved from Scotland to Northern Ireland. The Scotch-Irish, as they came to be known, were supposed to form a loyal British Protestant base in Catholic Ireland. But the British forbade them to export woolens in 1699 and pressured them to conform to the Anglican Church. These impositions, combined with excessive rents levied by Irish landowners, drove more than 200,000 Scotch-Irish to America by 1776.

The Scotch-Irish taught New Englanders the value of the ''Irish,'' or white, potato and the art of making fine linen from flax. Aggressively, conservatively Presbyterian, they showed no tolerance for other sects. Apart from literacy, necessary for Bible reading, they had little use for civilized airs or graces. Having come from a country where they were regarded as hostile foreigners, they adapted well to strife on the frontier. By 1750, Scotch-Irish settlements stretched for 700 miles along the Appalachians.

Both the Scotch-Irish and the Irish fought heroically for independence in the American Revolution. The Irish, nearly all Catholics who had felt the steely hand of British Protestantism, accounted for fully half of America's rebel army. In 1784 Lord Mountjoy, addressing the Irish Parliament, announced that England had "lost America through the exertions of Irish immigrants."

European wars kept farmers in Ireland prosperous until 1815, when peace returned and grain prices plummeted. Irish landlords promptly forced tenants off the land to make room for cattle, touching off the first huge wave of emigration. By 1845, 1.3 million Irish had fled to the United States. Those who stayed behind subsisted on potatoes. "A family of five or six would devour a barrel of potatoes a week," Bob Considine wrote in *It's the Irish*, "eating them three times a day with a little salt and washing them down with skimmed milk, if times were good."

According to the Dublin *Nation*, the potato harvest of 1845 showed "rich promise." Then one day the plants gave off a strange smell. Within 24 hours, said one witness, blight had left them "black as your shoe and burned to the clay." For the next five years, as Ireland twisted in the grip of famine, more than a million people left their homeland and farming forever.

The majority came to the cities of the Northeast and the roughest, most poorly paid work in industry and construction. Irishmen

Scotch-Irish laborers lay track and cable for the Broadway Surface Railroad at Union Square in New York. This wood engraving was published in Harper's Weekly *on September 26, 1891.*

Ironing was only one of the many tasks of the Irish domestic servant.

dug the Erie Canal. Gregarious, literate and witty, they actively pursued other jobs as they grew used to America: in politics, the priesthood, government and police work.

The Welsh, who began immigrating to America in earnest in the nineteenth century after a series of poor harvests, initially had a better time of it than the Irish. Wales was fifty years ahead of America in industry, and Welsh iron workers, miners and quarrymen had their pick of jobs until the late 1800s. Welsh immigration was very limited in size, but not in self-esteem. As one Welshman wrote: "We the Welsh are small in number but greater in our morality than anyone." Certainly they were as great in their appetites: a typical day included breakfast, midmorning lunch, dinner, midafternoon lunch, supper and a late evening meal. For those feeling pangs in between, the teapot, a loaf of bread and butter were always at hand.

Nineteenth-century Cornish immigrants also brought highly valued skills to America. Rightfully viewed as the aristocracy of the mining world, they at first roused the jealousy of fellow workers by making sure that job vacancies were filled by "Cousin Jacks" from Cornwall. They dug for iron, lead, copper, silver and gold from New Jersey to California, sometimes combining hardrock mining with farming, in traditional Cornish fashion. Cousin Jacks took comfort in Methodist Bible study, hearty drinking and the Cornish pasty, a mixture of meat, vegetables and fruit baked in a single crimped pastry envelope, which was designed to provide a decent meal at the bottom of a mine shaft. As the Cornish miners' toughness and a gift for a "plod" or tall tale made themselves known, "Cousin Jack" became a term of affection.

America warmed more slowly to the Scots, particularly since the terms "Scot" and "Tory" were interchangeable during the Revolution. When America won the war, many staunch Scottish Loyalists went home or to Canada. Those who remained, and the few Scots who continued to immigrate, felt that "Scotland might be the land of dreams, but Pennsylvania was the land of dollars." They settled in the northeast and the mid-Atlantic states and later in California, proving themselves vigorous and able farmers, merchants, professionals and craftsmen. The largest immigrant group from Scotland—300,000—came between 1921 and 1931 during a severe postwar depression. By then Americans had embraced several Scottish traditions: Halloween, New Year's Eve (hogmanay) and golf, introduced in 1818.

The twentieth century marked the decline of English immigration, which had never reached more than six figures in any decade. Numerical superiority, however, had ceased being important two centuries before. After 1690, the millions of immigrants who landed in America found a country irrevocably shaped by British law, language, religious theory and literature. The individual roots and histories of American citizens would emerge from the four corners of the earth, but America's national ancestry was firmly, unmistakably British.

Cranberry-picking was available work for recently arrived Scottish immigrants.

TEA SANDWICHES

6 TO 8 SERVINGS

CUCUMBER SANDWICHES

1   large cucumber
1/2   teaspoon salt
6   thin slices white bread, crusts removed
2   tablespoons mayonnaise
1   teaspoon finely chopped fresh parsley
     Freshly ground white pepper

Pare cucumber and cut lengthwise into quarters. Remove and discard seeds. Place cucumber in large bowl and sprinkle with salt. Add ice water to cover and let stand 15 minutes.

Drain cucumber and pat dry with paper towels. Using vegetable parer, cut lengthwise into paper-thin strips. Combine mayonnaise and parsley and spread about 1 teaspoonful evenly over each bread slice. Arrange cucumber strips over half the bread slices, cutting them to fit if necessary. Sprinkle lightly with pepper. Top with remaining bread slices, mayonnaise-side down. Cut each sandwich lengthwise into 4 strips and cover with clean damp towel. Refrigerate until needed.

WATERCRESS SANDWICHES

     Fresh watercress
2   tablespoons butter, softened
1   teaspoon fresh lemon juice
1   medium radish, finely chopped
     Pinch salt
6   thin slices whole wheat bread, crusts removed

Rinse watercress under cold running water. Discard stems and old leaves. Pat dry with paper towels. Blend butter, lemon juice, radish and salt. Spread slightly rounded teaspoonful of butter mixture over each bread slice. Arrange watercress in thin layer over half the bread slices and top with remaining slices, buttered-side down. Cut each sandwich diagonally into 4 triangles. Cover with clean damp towel and refrigerate until needed.

SMOKED SALMON SANDWICHES

2   tablespoons mayonnaise
1   teaspoon fresh lemon juice
1/2   teaspoon herb-flavored mustard
6   thin slices square pumpernickel or rye bread, crusts removed
2   to 3 ounces smoked salmon, sliced paper thin
     Freshly ground white pepper

Blend mayonnaise, lemon juice and mustard. Spread a slightly rounded teaspoonful over each bread slice. Arrange salmon in thin layer over half the slices and top with remaining slices, mayonnaise-side down. Sprinkle lightly with pepper. Cut each sandwich diagonally into 4 triangles. Cover with clean damp towel and refrigerate until needed.

PRECEDING OVERLEAF: *Delicate sandwiches, scones, crumpets and orange marmalade are necessary components of the proper English tea.*

POTTED SHRIMP

6 SERVINGS

16 tablespoons butter
1 pound shelled, cooked fresh tiny shrimp
    or 2 cups canned, drained
2 teaspoons fresh lemon juice
¼ teaspoon ground mace
¼ teaspoon ground nutmeg
⅛ teaspoon ground cayenne

TO SERVE:

Hot toast slices

Melt half the butter in medium saucepan over low heat. Remove from heat and stir in shrimp, lemon juice, mace, nutmeg and cayenne. Divide mixture equally among six 4- or 5-ounce soufflé dishes or custard cups.

Melt remaining butter in small saucepan over low heat. Skim off foam and discard. Spoon butter over shrimp mixture in dishes, discarding milky solids at bottom of saucepan. Cover dishes with plastic wrap and chill at least 6 hours or overnight. To serve, spread over hot toast.

CRUMPETS

10 TO 12

1 package active dry yeast (1 scant
    tablespoon)
1 teaspoon sugar
½ cup milk
5 tablespoons butter
½ teaspoon salt
1½ cups all-purpose flour
1 egg

Combine 6 tablespoons warm water (110° to 115° F.), yeast and sugar in large mixing bowl. Let stand until bubbly, about 5 minutes. Heat milk, 1 tablespoon butter and salt in small saucepan over low heat just until warm. Add to yeast mixture.

Add 1 cup flour to yeast mixture and beat until smooth, about 2 minutes on medium speed of electric mixer or 300 strokes by hand. Beat in egg. Add remaining flour and beat until smooth, about 1 minute. Cover batter with plastic wrap and let rise in warm place (80° to 85° F.) until doubled in bulk, about 1 hour.

Stir down batter and let rest 5 minutes. Meanwhile, melt remaining butter in small saucepan over low heat. Skim off foam and discard milky solids from bottom of saucepan. Brush bottom of heavy 10- or 12-inch skillet with melted butter. Brush insides of four crumpet rings or 3-inch round cookie cutters with butter and place rings in skillet.

Heat skillet over medium heat. Spoon about 2 tablespoons batter into each ring. (If batter is too thick to spread evenly to fill rings, stir in 1 to 2 tablespoons water, as needed.)

Cook until batter begins to bubble on top and is lightly browned on bottom, about 2 minutes. Remove rings. Using pancake turner, turn crumpets over. Cook until lightly browned on bottom and done in centers, 2 to 3 minutes longer. Place crumpets in basket or on serving plate. Cover to keep warm while cooking remaining batter. Serve hot. Or, cool slightly, split horizontally into halves and toast before serving.

BLUEBERRY TEA SCONES

1½ DOZEN

2   cups all-purpose flour
⅓   cup sugar
2   teaspoons baking powder
½   teaspoon salt
5½   tablespoons butter, chilled
¾   cup fresh or frozen blueberries
1   egg
1   egg yolk
⅓   to ½ cup milk
1   teaspoon grated lemon rind
1   egg white
     Sugar

Stir together flour, sugar, baking powder and salt. Cut in butter with pastry blender or 2 knives until mixture resembles coarse crumbs. Stir in blueberries. Blend egg, egg yolk, ⅓ cup milk and lemon rind. Add to flour mixture, stirring just until flour

is moistened. Add more milk, if necessary, to make a soft dough.

Turn dough onto lightly floured surface and knead gently 30 seconds. Roll or pat dough out to ½-inch thickness using cookie cutter or rim of glass, cut dough into 2-inch circles. Place circles 1 inch apart on ungreased baking sheet. Re-roll and cut out scraps of dough. Beat egg white with fork until frothy and brush evenly over circles. Sprinkle lightly with sugar. Bake in preheated 425°F. oven until golden, 12 to 15 minutes. Transfer wire rack and cool 5 to 10 minutes before serving.

NOTE: For plain tea scones, eliminate blueberries and lemon rind.

RICHMOND MAIDS OF HONOUR

16 TARTS

2   cups all-purpose flour
½   cup plus 1 tablespoon sugar
1   teaspoon salt
5½   tablespoons butter, chilled
⅓   cup lard or vegetable shortening
3   egg yolks
½   cup ground almonds
2   tablespoons fine dry bread crumbs
1   teaspoon grated lemon rind
1   teaspoon fresh lemon juice
¼   cup heavy cream

Combine flour, 1 tablespoon sugar and salt in medium bowl. Cut in butter and lard with pastry blender or 2 knives until mixture resembles coarse crumbs. Sprinkle 6 to 8 tablespoons ice water over flour mixture, mixing lightly with fork just until dough sticks together. Press dough into ball. Roll out on lightly floured surface to about ¼-inch thickness. Using floured 3-inch cookie cutter or rim of glass, cut out 16 circles of dough. Re-roll and cut out scraps of dough. Fit circles into flour-dusted 2½-inch muffin cups, pressing firmly against sides of cups (dough will not completely fill sides).

Beat egg yolks and remaining sugar in medium bowl with whisk until lemon colored, 1 to 2 minutes. Beat in almonds, bread crumbs, lemon rind and juice, then gradually beat in cream. Spoon about 1 tablespoon egg-almond mixture into each pastry-lined muffin cup. Bake in preheated 400°F. oven until filling is golden, 15 to 20 minutes. Transfer tarts to wire racks. Cool to room temperature.

WELSH RAREBIT

6 SERVINGS

12   slices homemade-style white bread, crusts removed
4   cups (1 pound) shredded sharp Cheddar cheese
1   tablespoon cornstarch
½   cup beer or ale
1½   teaspoons Worcestershire sauce
1   teaspoon prepared English-style mustard
½   teaspoon curry powder
     Pinch cayenne
1   egg yolk
     Paprika

Toast bread until golden. Arrange 2 slices in each of 6 ramekins or other shallow ovenproof dishes.

Toss cheese and cornstarch together until cheese is completely coated. Place cheese, beer, Worcestershire sauce, mustard, curry powder and cayenne in 1 ½-quart saucepan. Heat over medium-low heat, stirring constantly, until mixture is bubbly, about 5 minutes. Beat egg yolk slightly with fork in small bowl and blend in 2 or 3 tablespoons hot cheese mixture. Stir yolk mixture into cheese mixture until blended.

Spread about 2 tablespoons cheese mixture over toast in ramekins. Sprinkle with paprika. Broil 4 inches from heat until cheese is lightly browned, 1 to 2 minutes. Serve immediately.

TRIFLE

6 TO 8 SERVINGS

Butter Sponge Cake (recipe follows)
¼ *cup apricot preserves*
¼ *cup raspberry preserves*
½ *cup pale dry sherry*
2 *to 4 tablespoons brandy or cognac*
Vanilla Custard (recipe follows)
1 *to 2 cups fresh raspberries, if available*
¼ *cup sliced blanched almonds, toasted*
1 *cup heavy cream, whipped*

Prepare *Butter Sponge Cake*. Cool and cut in half horizontally. Spread one half evenly with apricot preserves and the other with raspberry preserves. Cut halves into strips 1½ inch wide and 3 inches long. Arrange half the strips, preserve-side up in alternate flavors, in 2-quart clear glass bowl. Sprinkle with ¼ cup sherry and half the brandy. Arrange remaining strips, preserve-side up, on large plate and sprinkle with remaining sherry and brandy. Let stand 30 minutes.

Sprinkle half the raspberries and half the almonds over cake strips in glass bowl. Top with half the *Vanilla Custard*. Repeat layers with reserved strips, remaining raspberries, almonds and custard. Garnish with whipped cream. Serve within 30 minutes. (Refrigerate if not served immediately.)

BUTTER SPONGE CAKE

1 *cup all-purpose flour, sifted*
1 *teaspoon baking powder*
¼ *teaspoon salt*
⅓ *cup milk*
4 *tablespoons butter*
2 *eggs*
¾ *cup sugar*
1 *teaspoon grated lemon rind*
1 *teaspoon vanilla extract*

Sift together flour, baking powder and salt in small mixing bowl. Heat milk and butter in small saucepan over medium-low heat until butter melts (do not allow milk to boil). Remove from heat.

Beat eggs in small mixer bowl until thick and lemon-colored, about 3 minutes at high speed of electric mixer. Gradually beat in sugar and beat 3

Topped with fresh raspberries and thick whipped cream, this magnificent Trifle *is served in a Georgian crystal bowl.*

to 4 minutes longer.

Add flour mixture and beat just until smooth. Beat in milk mixture, lemon rind and vanilla just until blended. Pour batter into greased and floured 9-inch square baking pan. Bake in preheated 350°F. oven until cake tests done, about 25 minutes. Cool cake 10 minutes in pan on wire rack. Remove cake from pan and cool completely on wire rack.

VANILLA CUSTARD

1¹/₂	cups milk
1	cup heavy cream
3	tablespoons sugar
2	teaspoons cornstarch
3	eggs
1	teaspoon vanilla extract

Measure milk and cream into 1 ½-quart saucepan. Stir sugar and cornstarch together in small bowl until completely mixed. Blend into milk mixture. Cook over medium-low heat, stirring frequently, until mixture thickens and boils, about 15 minutes. Remove from heat.

Beat eggs in medium bowl until frothy. Whisk in about ½ cup hot milk mixture until blended. Stir egg mixture into milk mixture in saucepan. Bring to boil over medium heat, stirring constantly. Boil 1 minute. Remove from heat and stir in vanilla. Cover with plastic wrap directly over custard, until ready to use.

STEAK AND KIDNEY PIE

6 SERVINGS

¹/₂	pound beef kidney
3	teaspoons salt
1¹/₂	pounds round steak
¹/₃	cup all-purpose flour
¹/₄	teaspoon freshly ground black pepper
3	tablespoons butter
1	tablespoon vegetable oil
¹/₂	cup chopped onion
¹/₂	pound mushrooms, cleaned and sliced
1¹/₂	cups rich homemade beef broth
1	tablespoon chopped fresh parsley
1	tablespoon tomato paste
2	teaspoons Worcestershire sauce
¹/₂	teaspoon dried thyme, crumbled
1	small bay leaf
¹/₄	cup pale dry sherry or dry red wine
	Pastry (recipe follows)

1	egg yolk
1	tablespoon milk

Peel off and discard membrane from kidney. Trim and discard any fat. Cut kidney into 1-inch cubes. Combine 4 cups water and 2 teaspoons salt in large bowl, add kidney and let stand 30 minutes.

Trim and discard any fat from beef. Cut meat into 1-inch cubes. Pat beef dry with paper towels. Combine flour, remaining salt and pepper. Dredge beef in flour mixture to coat evenly.

Sauté half the cubes in butter and

The delicious aroma of Steak and Kidney Pie *is released when its golden crust is gently broken.*

oil in large skillet over medium-high heat, turning frequently, until browned on all sides, 8 to 10 minutes. Transfer cooked beef to deep 2-quart casserole, then brown second batch.

Drain kidney, pat dry with paper towels and dredge in flour mixture. Sauté in remaining butter mixture in skillet, turning frequently until cubes are evenly browned, 8 to 10 minutes. Add to beef in casserole.

Sauté onion and mushrooms in butter mixture remaining in skillet, stirring frequently, until onions are soft, about 5 minutes. Add to casserole. Discard fat from skillet. Place broth, parsley, tomato paste, Worcestershire sauce, thyme and bay leaf in skillet. Cook over medium heat, stirring frequently, until mixture boils, about 5 minutes. Remove from heat and stir in sherry. Pour over meat mixture in casserole.

Roll out pastry dough on lightly floured surface to ¼-inch thickness. Cut ½-inch wide strips from around edges of dough. Arrange strips, overlapping slightly, around rim of casserole. Press firmly into place. Brush strips lightly with water. Arrange remaining pastry dough on top of casserole. Trim off excess with sharp knife. Press dough firmly into strips on rim of casserole, using tines of fork. Reroll scraps of dough, if desired, and cut into decorative shapes.

Beat egg yolk and milk together in small bowl. Brush over pastry. Arrange decorative shapes on top and brush with egg mixture. Cut several 1-inch slashes through pastry.

Bake in preheated 425°F. oven 30 minutes. Reduce oven temperature to 350°F. and bake until crust is golden, about 30 minutes longer. Serve immediately.

PASTRY

2   cups sifted all-purpose flour
½   teaspoon salt
8   tablespoons chilled butter, cut into pieces
3   tablespoons chilled vegetable shortening

Combine flour and salt in medium bowl. Using pastry blender or 2 knives, cut in butter and shortening until mixture resembles coarse crumbs. Sprinkle with about 5 tablespoons ice water, 1 tablespoon at a time, mixing lightly with fork just until all flour is moistened and dough sticks together. Add additional 1 tablespoon water if needed. Press dough firmly into ball. Wrap in plastic wrap and refrigerate about two hours.

CORNISH PASTIES

10 TO 12

4   cups all-purpose flour
2   teaspoons salt
1   cup lard, chilled
8   tablespoons butter, chilled
1   pound lean boneless top round
1½   cups chopped pared potatoes
¾   cup chopped onion
¾   cup chopped pared turnips
1   large carrot, pared and chopped
¼   teaspoon freshly ground black pepper
1   egg, beaten

Combine flour and 1 teaspoon salt in large bowl. Cut in lard and butter with pastry blender or 2 knives until mixture resembles coarse crumbs. Sprinkle ¾ to 1 cup ice water over flour mixture, mixing lightly with fork just until dough sticks together (add just enough water as needed to form dough). Divide dough into 3 equal portions and shape each into ball. Wrap in plastic wrap and refrigerate 1 hour. Freeze meat 30 to 45 minutes. Chop finely, then cover.

Roll out each portion of dough on lightly floured surface to ⅛-inch thickness. With sharp knife, cut dough into 7-inch circles, using inverted plate or bowl as guide. Reroll and cut out scraps of dough.

Combine meat and all remaining ingredients except egg in large bowl. Toss to mix. Spoon rounded ⅓ cup measure of meat mixture onto center of each pastry circle. Brush water lightly around edges of each circle. Fold over to form semicircles, or bring edges of pastry together over top of filling. Pinch dough together all around edges to seal in filling. Place pastries on greased baking sheet and brush evenly with beaten egg. Using sharp knife, cut 2 1-inch slits in top of each pastry.

Bake in preheated 400°F. oven 15 minutes. Reduce oven temperature to 350°F.; continue baking until pastries are golden, about 30 minutes longer. Serve hot or at room temperature.

YORKSHIRE PUDDING

6 SERVINGS

1   cup milk
1   cup all-purpose flour
2   eggs
¼   teaspoon salt
     Pinch of freshly ground white pepper
3   tablespoons roast beef drippings or
     melted lard or butter

Combine all ingredients except drippings in 5-cup blender container. Blend 5 seconds. Scrape down sides of container and blend until smooth,

35 to 40 seconds longer. Cover batter and refrigerate 1 hour.

Pour drippings into 13 × 9 × 2-inch flameproof baking pan. Heat on range over medium heat until drippings sizzle. Blend chilled batter 5 seconds, then pour into pan. Bake in preheated 425°F. oven 15 minutes. Reduce heat to 375°F. and continue baking until pudding is golden and puffy around edges, 15 to 20 minutes longer. Serve hot.

IRISH SODA BREAD

1 LOAF

1½ cups all-purpose flour
1 cup whole wheat flour
1 teaspoon baking soda
½ teaspoon salt
¼ cup currants
1¼ to 1½ cups buttermilk
1 tablespoon butter, melted

Combine flour, baking soda and salt in large mixing bowl. Stir in currants. Add 1 ¼ cups buttermilk and stir just until dry ingredients are moistened. (Add more buttermilk, if necessary, to make a soft dough.) Turn dough onto lightly floured surface and knead gently 1 to 2 minutes. Shape into ball and place on greased baking sheet. Pat into 8-inch circle. Using sharp knife or razor blade, cut ½-inch-deep "X" in top of dough.

Bake in preheated 425°F. oven until golden, about 45 minutes. Transfer to wire rack and brush with melted butter. Serve hot or at room temperature.

BUBBLE AND SQUEAK

6 SERVINGS

1 medium onion, chopped
3 tablespoons bacon drippings or butter
2½ cups cooked shredded cabbage (about 1 pound)
2 cups mashed potatoes (about 1 pound)
1 cup chopped leftover cooked beef or corned beef (optional)
½ teaspoon salt
⅛ teaspoon freshly ground black pepper

TO SERVE:
Wow-Wow Sauce (recipe follows)

Cook onion in bacon drippings in 10-inch skillet over medium heat until soft, about 5 minutes. Place cabbage in colander and press with back of large spoon to remove excess liquid. Add cabbage to onions and stir in potatoes. Cook, stirring frequently, until vegetables begin to brown, about 5 minutes. Stir in meat if desired and salt and pepper. Continue cooking without stirring until golden on bot-

Currants and buttermilk are the special ingredients in crusty Irish Soda Bread.

tom, about 10 minutes. Invert mixture onto large serving plate. Cover with foil and keep warm in 225°F. oven while preparing *Wow-Wow Sauce*. Cut Bubble and Squeak into wedges. Serve hot with wow-wow sauce.

WOW-WOW SAUCE

2   tablespoons butter
2   tablespoons minced onion
2   tablespoons all-purpose flour
1   cup rich homemade beef broth
1   tablespoon white wine vinegar
1   tablespoon Worcestershire sauce
1   tablespoon English-style mustard
½   teaspoon prepared horseradish
¼   teaspoon salt
⅛   teaspoon freshly ground black pepper
2   tablespoons finely chopped fresh parsley

Melt butter in 1½-quart saucepan over medium heat. Stir in onion. Cook, stirring constantly, until onion is soft but not browned, about 3 minutes. Stir in flour and cook 1 minute, stirring constantly. Add broth all at once and whisk until smooth. Stir in all remaining ingredients except parsley. Bring to boil. Reduce heat to medium-low and simmer, stirring frequently, until sauce is thickened, about 10 minutes. Stir in parsley.

COCK-A-LEEKIE SOUP

10 TO 12 SERVINGS

1   stewing chicken (5 to 6 pounds)
6   large leeks, thoroughly washed
1   medium onion, peeled and chopped
2   large carrots, pared and chopped
1   cup pearl barley
2   teaspoons salt
¼   teaspoon freshly ground white pepper
4   sprigs fresh parsley
12   whole peppercorns
3   whole cloves
2   bay leaves
1   teaspoon dried thyme
¼   cup chopped fresh parsley

Rinse chicken under cold running water. Place chicken in 8- to 10-quart stockpot. Add 3 quarts water.

Cut leeks crosswise into ½-inch slices, including 2 inches of green tops. Add to pot with onion, carrots, barley, salt, white pepper and herbs, tied in cheesecloth bag. Bring to boil over high heat. Reduce heat to low. Simmer, partially covered, until chicken is very tender, about 3 hours. Skim off and discard foam that appears on top during cooking.

When chicken is cooked, place it on large platter. Let stand until cool enough to handle. Remove skin and pull meat off bones. Discard skin and bones. Cut meat into bite-sized pieces. Return to pot. Simmer 5 minutes longer. Skim off fat from top. Discard herb bag. Serve soup hot, sprinkled with parsley.

LEFT: Bubble and Squeak *is best served with a tangy* Wow-Wow Sauce.
OVERLEAF: *Chicken and leeks are essentials of the Scottish* Cock-A-Leekie Soup.

Eastern Europe

Polish Easter Menu

Zakaski (Hors d'Oeuvres)
Chlodnick (Cold Beet and Cucumber Soup)
Mizerja Ze Smietana (Cucumbers in Sour Cream)
Kielbasa (Polish Garlic Sausage) with Kapusta (Sauerkraut)
Sztufada (Braised Beef)
Babka Wielkanocna (Polish Easter Bread)
Tea and Coffee

RECOMMENDED WINES

Chenin Blanc
Gewurztraminer
Merlot

Additional Recipes

Pörkölt (Stewed Pork), Hungary
Satsivi (Fish with Walnut Sauce), Russia
Paprikas Csirke (Chicken Paprika), Hungary
Ghivetch (Rumanian Mixed Vegetables), Rumania
Pierogi (Filled "Pockets"), Poland
Bigos (Hunter's Stew), Poland
Apfelstrudel (Apple Strudel), Hungary

They had no country of their own to leave behind, because their land had been divided
among Russia, Germany and Austria; they arrived to face American prejudice that would
force them to create a separate, protective national identity, a country within a country. But
the Poles who sold their possessions and livestock to sail west were
dogged realists. They had been raised on folk tales that promised
success to those who worked for it. By 1914, more than 2.5 million
Poles, nearly all peasants, had come through Ellis Island, prepared to perform their own miracles.

The end of the nineteenth century found most of Eastern Europe, including Russia, Austria, Rumania and Hungary, trying to
sustain a population explosion on an antiquated system of land
division. "Over there was rough," recalled Vera Gurchikov, who
left Eastern Europe in 1911. "No meat in the old country, not like
here. We ate potatoes, cabbage, beans. We lived in a little house,
the roof made out of straw, one room." Armies of peasants hired
out as day laborers on farms or in urban industries.

The Poles, who placed great significance on land ownership,
smoldered with the desire to control their own ground and lives.
"Old Europe knew them as a fearsomely proud and independent
people," W.S. Kuniczak wrote in *My Name Is Million*. "Rapacious
neighbors could swallow their country but never digest them."

As Eastern Europe's economic problems burgeoned, news
about life in America flowed into crowded villages, some of it de-
livered by agents for steamship lines, still more by mail. Polish
immigrants regarded letter-writing as a duty. Most needed the
help of a *pisennik*, or scribe, but their characteristically honest ac-
counts forged "immigration chains" whose links numbered in the

*The firm, direct gaze of this Slavic woman
was characteristic of the determination
shown by millions of Eastern European
immigrants.*

This Eastern European immigrant stands ready to face the challenges of a new life in America.

thousands.

"In America, you will spill more sweat in one day than in a week back home," they wrote. "Here they pick out their workmen like cattle at the market. . . But I would not go back if someone was to give me the master's estate. God's truth, when I remember the misery at home my skin crawls."

"Dear Sister: I'll send you a *shiffkarta* [one-way ticket], because back home you're serving others from childhood, and so it will be until your old age, but in America you can make something of yourself."

Polish men in the prime of life arrived first. Knowledgeable about farming but little else, they reached the United States when its energies had turned from homesteading to industry. That left them one commodity to sell: endurance. They brought it to coal, iron and copper mines; to steel, textile and lumber mills; to slaughterhouses and meat-packing plants. They lived in boardinghouses run by Czechs or Germans, paying $2 or $3 a month, sending home two-thirds of their income (which in 1900 averaged $1.50 a day). Then they sent for their families, or for brides.

"Girls in America are lazy and let themselves go, so send me Zoska."

"Dear Cousin: I'm happy that old Mrs. Kalinowska is bringing me a pretty girl, but maybe she can bring two? Because, you see, there's two of us bachelors here, and we'd both like to marry. . . ."

One photograph of Polish brides-to-be on the deck of a steamship catches them looking sideways from under their scarves and smiling. Because American employers regarded them as the strongest and most cheerful component of the female labor force, Polish women found themselves washing dishes or scrubbing floors fifteen hours a day, or working at the heaviest jobs in cotton, twine, tobacco or garment factories. Many broke down under the strain. Many more returned each night to homes and families they managed on the scantiest of budgets, raising thrift to an art form, waiting for the day they could buy land of their own.

For Poles who worked in cities, their homes created the illusion of country life. Most families planted gardens and even kept a cow, goat or chickens. "It was a rare Polish section in an American city where front yards were not full of flowers, and where an apple or pear tree did not grow behind the house among sweet peas, tomatoes, onions, cabbages, carrots and potatoes," notes Kuniczak. Home-grown produce, added to a diet of inexpensive cuts of pork and beef, smoked fish and dark bread, kept costs down. So did the income from the boarders Polish women took in for as little as 15 cents a week.

The Polish stamina and patience, qualities that made an incalculable contribution to America's growth in the early twentieth century, were both abused and insulted. In a fierce response to prejudice, Poles began to shape and protect their national identity as they never had in Europe. When their children were ridiculed for their parents' stoicism in grueling jobs, Poles created more than 400 schools of their own. Devoutly Catholic, but excluded from Irish-American Catholicism, they wrung money from substandard incomes and built handsome churches and basilicas, where they offered Mass in Polish. Irish-American powers in the church denounced the practice as foreign and attempted to replace Polish priests with Irish ones. The Poles, notably one Bishop Hodur, responded by risking excommunication and forming the Polish National Church, which was eventually recognized by the Vatican.

Bit by bit, the *za chlebem* ("for bread") immigrants scratched out

Like thousands of Polish immigrants, this couple waits at Ellis Island with all their worldly possessions.

Polish workers leave the mine shaft in a Pennsylvania coal mine.

a niche in America. For inspiration, they thought of Thaddeus Kosciuscko and Casimir Pulaski, Polish patriots who fought in the American Revolution; Dr. Maria Elizabeth Zakrzewska, who in the late 1880s founded two hospitals for and staffed exclusively by women, as well as the first American school for professional nurses; and Ernestine Potowska, who persuaded the New York State Legislature to enact the nation's first law giving married women property rights. Ignacy Jan Paderewski, the pianist, composer, statesman and Polish hero, roared across the American plains in his private railroad car, inspiring both Poles and Americans, including President Woodrow Wilson, with a combination of Chopin and eloquent speeches on the restoration of the Polish nation.

Armed with a growing feeling of self-worth and strong sense of justice, Polish-Americans became courageous fighters for workers' rights. Casimir Kopek, who immigrated in 1910, expressed the underlying motivation: "I never keep anybody in slavery. I *was* slave!" Throughout the massive, often violent labor struggles that marked the early part of the century, more than half a million Poles risked their jobs and sometimes their lives to stand by fellow workers.

They fought not against the American system, but for it. When Wilson called for volunteers during World War I, 40,000 of the first 100,000 men reporting for duty were Poles. They knew that they might meet relatives fighting for Austria in the trenches, but they simply said, "I go if you need me." Polish working men and women pledged more money to the Third Liberty Loan than any other community did. By 1918, Wilson included an independent Poland in his program for peace.

Slowly, tenaciously, Polish peasants in America continued to approach success through hard work. They moved from miners' shanties to neatly tended neighborhoods and farms. They sent their children to work, but also to school for a privilege they had mistrusted in their European employers: literacy. The lesson of self-reliance kept their expectations alive and growing from generation to generation.

"I work many hundreds of feet under the ground," wrote the miner who sent for Zoska. "Don't see God's sun from morning to night for those 2 dollars they give me. . . . (But) who can't make a life for himself in this country, will never do it anywhere else."

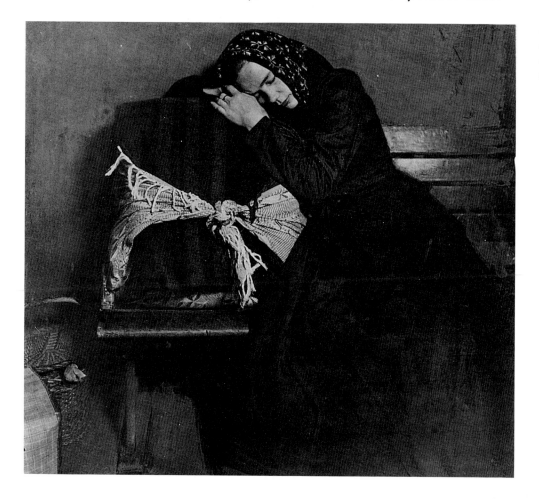

After an exhausting passage and an exciting arrival, this young Bohemian immigrant takes a brief rest on Ellis Island in a photograph by Lewis W. Hine.

ZAKASKI

Hors d'Oeuvres

Zakaski is the name given to an un-limited variety of delightful tidbits served as the introductory course in a Polish dinner.

Because they are designed to stim-ulate the eye and thus whet the appe-tite, particular care is taken to make the presentation as attractive as possi-ble. Zakaski may be served buffet-fashion, arranged on platters and passed before dinner or offered to guests at the table before the soup course.

A typical zakaski might include a variety of cooked and smoked cold fish, cold meats, cheese, relishes, marinated or pickled vegetables, stuffed eggs and assorted breads with flavored butters. A few examples are:

Pickled mushrooms
Anchovy fillets
Picked onions
Smoked oysters, clams or mussels
Assorted cheeses (Tybo, Danbo,
*   Samsoe, Danish Blue, Esrom,*
*   Danish Fontina or Havarti)*
Cold smoked salmon or whitefish
Olives
Sliced cold chicken or tongue
Sliced pumpernickel or rye bread

CHLODNIK

Cold Beet and Cucumber Soup
8 SERVINGS

1	*pound medium beets, including tops*
1/4	*cup dry red wine*
2	*tablespoons cider vinegar*
2	*teaspoons salt*
1 1/2	*cups dairy sour cream*
1	*pound shrimp, cooked, shelled and deveined*
2	*medium cucumbers, pared, seeded and chopped*
4	*radishes, thinly sliced*
4	*green onions (including tops), thinly sliced*
3	*tablespoons lemon juice*
1	*tablespoon chopped fresh dill*

FOR GARNISH:

1	*lemon, thinly sliced*
2	*hard-cooked eggs, finely chopped*

Pare beets, shred coarsely and place in 3-quart saucepan. Clean tops thor-oughly, pat dry with paper towels and chop finely. Add to beets along with 6 cups water, wine, vinegar and salt. Heat to boiling over high heat. Re-duce heat to low. Cook beets, partial-ly covered, until tender, about 15

PRECEDING OVERLEAF: *In Chlodnik, shrimp, cucumbers and beets are combined for a refreshing cold soup.*

minutes. Drain beets, reserving liquid. Let stand until cooled.

Thoroughly blend sour cream into beet liquid in large glass bowl. Stir in beets, shrimp, cucumbers, radishes, onions, lemon juice and dill. Cover with plastic wrap and refrigerate until chilled, about 2 hours. Serve cold, garnished with lemon slices and chopped egg.

MIZERJA ZE SMIETANA

Cucumbers in Sour Cream
6 SERVINGS

2   large cucumbers (about 1½ pounds),
    pared and thinly sliced
    Salt
1   *cup dairy sour cream*
2   *tablespoons white vinegar*
1   *tablespoon chopped fresh dill*
2   *teaspoons sugar*
⅛   *teaspoon freshly ground white pepper*

Layer cucumber slices, salting each layer lightly, in medium-sized glass bowl. Cover with heavy plate. Let stand 2 hours.

Drain cucumbers, squeezing out as much liquid as possible. Pat dry with paper towels. Place cucumbers in glass bowl. Combine sour cream, vinegar, dill, sugar and pepper and stir into cucumbers. Refrigerate at least 1 hour before serving.

KIELBASA

Polish Garlic Sausage
3 POUNDS

    Natural hog casings
2   *pounds boneless pork butt, coarsely*
    ground
1   *pound boneless beef chuck, coarsely*
    ground
1   *to 2 ounces pork fat, cut into ½-inch*
    cubes
1   *large onion, grated*
3   *cloves garlic, minced*
1   *tablespoon chopped fresh parsley*
1½ *teaspoons salt*
1   *teaspoon dried marjoram, crumbled*
1   *teaspoon dried sage, crumbled*

1   *teaspoon mustard seeds*
½   *teaspoon dried thyme, crumbled*
½   *teaspoon freshly ground black pepper*
¼   *teaspoon freshly ground nutmeg*
2   *tablespoons butter*

TO SERVE:

    Kapusta (recipe follows)

Rinse casings under warm running water. Place in small bowl, cover with warm water and let stand 10 minutes. Insert 2 fingers into one end of each casing, hold under warm running water and let water run through. Tie knot in one end of each casing and place on paper towels.

Grind meats and pork fat together using fine blade of food grinder or process in food processor fitted with steel blade. Transfer meat to large bowl and add onion, garlic, seasonings and ½ cup cold water. Mix thoroughly. (If using food processor, add onions, garlic, seasonings and ½ cup cold water to ground meat mixture in work bowl and process, using on/off technique, until well mixed, 10 to 15 seconds.)

To stuff casing by hand, slip open end of each casing over tube of large funnel and work casing onto tube until knotted end is about 1 inch from mouth of tube. Press meat mixture through funnel into casing, filling loosely. As casings are filled, twist and tie off 18- to 20-inch lengths, using heavy thread. If air pockets develop in sausage, pierce casing with needle.

If sausage will not be cooked immediately, wrap and refrigerate. Use within 2 days. Uncooked sausage may be frozen.

To cook kielbasa, coil 1 or 2 lengths to fit large skillet and add water to cover. Cover and heat to simmering over medium-high heat. Reduce heat to low and simmer until kielbasa is cooked through, about 10 minutes.

Drain water from skillet and add butter. Cook kielbasa over medium heat until browned, 4 to 5 minutes on each side. Serve hot with *Kapusta*.

NOTE: To fill casing with food grinder or mixer, follow manufacturer's instructions.

KAPUSTA

Sauerkraut
6 SERVINGS

2   pounds fresh sauerkraut
2   tablespoons butter
½   cup rich homemade beef broth
½   cup dry white wine
1   medium tomato, peeled, seeded and
        chopped
1   medium onion, chopped
⅛   teaspoon freshly ground black pepper

Rinse sauerkraut with cold running water. Drain and squeeze out as much liquid as possible. Melt butter in large skillet over medium heat and add sauerkraut, broth, wine, tomato, onion and pepper. Cover and heat to simmering, then reduce heat to low. Simmer, covered, until onion is soft, about 10 minutes.

SZTUFADA

Braised Beef

6 TO 8 SERVINGS

1	large onion, sliced
8	whole peppercorns
4	large bay leaves
1/2	teaspoon ground allspice
2/3	cup dry red wine
1/3	cup cider vinegar
3	pounds beef rump or round
2	teaspoons dried marjoram, crumbled
2	tablespoons butter
1	tablespoon vegetable oil
2/3	cup rich homemade beef broth
3	tablespoons tomato paste
1	clove garlic, finely chopped
1/4	teaspoon freshly ground black pepper

Combine 2 cups water, onion, peppercorns, bay leaves and allspice in medium saucepan and bring to boil over high heat. Boil until onion is soft, about 3 minutes. Remove from heat and stir in 1/3 cup of the wine and the vinegar. Cool to room temperature.

Rub beef with 1 teaspoon of the marjoram and place in large glass bowl. Pour cooled wine mixture over meat. Cover with plastic wrap and refrigerate 1 to 2 days, turning meat occasionally.

Drain meat, discarding marinade. Pat meat dry with paper towels. Brown meat in butter and oil in 10-inch skillet over medium-high heat, 4 to 5 minutes on each side. Combine broth, remaining wine, tomato paste, garlic, remaining marjoram and pepper and pour over meat. Reduce heat to low. Cover and cook until meat is tender, 1½ to 2 hours. Slice and serve hot with pan juices.

BABKA WIELKANOCNA

Polish Easter Bread

1 LOAF

9	tablespoons butter, softened
8	tablespoons sugar
4	egg yolks
1	package (1/4 ounce) active dry yeast (1 scant tablespoon)
1	teaspoon salt
1	teaspoon grated lemon rind
1	teaspoon grated orange rind
1/2	teaspoon ground cinnamon

1	cup milk
4	cups all-purpose flour, plus additional 1/4 cup as needed
1	cup golden raisins
2	tablespoons fine dry bread crumbs

Beat 8 tablespoons of the butter and 7 tablespoons of the sugar in large mixer bowl at high speed of electric mixer until light and fluffy, about 5 minutes. Add egg yolks and beat until lemon colored, about 5 minutes.

Meanwhile, combine ¼ cup warm water (110° to 115°F.), remaining sugar and yeast, stirring to dissolve yeast. Let stand until bubbly, about 5 minutes.

Blend yeast mixture, salt, lemon and orange rind and cinnamon into egg mixture until smooth. Alternately beat in milk and enough flour to make a soft dough, then stir in raisins.

Knead dough in bowl until no long-er sticky, about 5 minutes. Let stand in warm place (80° to 85°F.) until doubled in bulk, about 1½ hours.

Stir down dough. Butter a 3-quart fluted tube pan with remaining 1 tablespoon butter, sprinkle with crumbs and rotate pan to coat bottom and sides evenly. Spoon dough into pan and cover with plastic wrap. Let stand in warm place until doubled in bulk, about 1½ hours.

Bake in preheated 350°F. oven until browned, 25 to 30 minutes. Cool 5 minutes in pan, then invert bread onto cooling rack. Cool completely.

PÖRKÖLT

Stewed Pork

6 SERVINGS

2   cups chopped onions
1   large clove garlic, finely chopped
4   tablespoons butter
1½ tablespoons sweet Hungarian paprika
2   pounds boneless pork, cut into 1½-inch
       cubes
½   cup rich homemade chicken broth
2   medium ripe tomatoes, peeled, seeded
       and chopped
2   tablespoons tomato paste
1   large green pepper, seeded and cut into
       thin strips
½   teaspoon salt
¼   teaspoon freshly ground black pepper

TO SERVE:

Galuskas (recipe follows)

Sauté onions and garlic in butter in 10-inch skillet over medium heat, stirring frequently, until onion is light brown, about 10 minutes. Remove from heat and stir in paprika until onion is evenly coated. Stir in pork and stock and return to heat. Reduce heat to low, cover and simmer 30 minutes.

Stir tomatoes and tomato paste into pork mixture. Cover and cook 15 minutes. Stir in green pepper, salt and pepper. Cook, uncovered, until pork is tender, about 15 minutes longer.

Prepare Galuskas. Drain and spoon onto serving platter. Top with Pörkölt. Serve hot.

GALUSKAS

3   cups all-purpose flour
2½ teaspoons salt
3   eggs

Combine flour and ½ teaspoon of the salt in large mixing bowl. Beat in eggs with wooden spoon or electric mixer with dough hook. Beat in enough cold water (5 to 7 tablespoons) to make moderately stiff dough.

Knead dough on lightly floured surface until small blisters form just below surface, 8 to 10 minutes. Cover dough and let stand 1 hour.

Break off pieces of dough about the size of small eggs, roll between palms and work surface into ropes about ½ inch in diameter. Cut crosswise into ½-inch pieces and place in single layer on cookie sheet.

Combine 3 quarts water and remaining 2 teaspoons salt in greased 5-quart Dutch oven. Heat to boiling. Drop dough, about 2 dozen pieces at a time, into boiling water. Cook until dumplings rise to top, 2 to 4 minutes. Remove with slotted spoon and drain.

ABOVE: *Similar to goulash,* Pörkölt, *is flavored with the indispensable paprika.*

SATSIVI

Fish with Walnut Sauce
4 SERVINGS

2 pounds fresh sturgeon, whitefish or sole
  fillets
2 tablespoons butter, melted
3/4 teaspoon salt
1/4 teaspoon freshly ground white pepper
2 tablespoons finely chopped onion
1 small clove garlic, finely chopped
1 tablespoon butter
3/4 cup rich homemade chicken broth
1 tablespoon white wine vinegar
2 teaspoons finely chopped fresh parsley
1/4 teaspoon dried basil, crumbled
1/4 teaspoon ground coriander
1/8 teaspoon powdered saffron
1/2 cup walnuts (2 ounces), ground

Place fish in single layer in greased baking dish and brush with melted butter. Sprinkle with 1/2 teaspoon of the salt and 1/8 teaspoon of the pepper. Bake in preheated 500°F. oven until fish flakes easily when tested with a fork, 5 to 10 minutes (allow 5 minutes for each 1/2-inch thickness).

Meanwhile, sauté onion and garlic in remaining 1 tablespoon butter in small saucepan over medium heat until soft, about 5 minutes. Stir in remaining ingredients. Boil stirring, until sauce is slightly thickened, about 3 to 5 minutes. Spoon sauce over fish. Serve hot or cold.

PAPRIKAS CSIRKE

Chicken Paprika
4 SERVINGS

1 broiler/fryer chicken (about 3 pounds),
  cut into serving pieces
  Salt
  Freshly ground black pepper
2 tablespoons butter
1 tablespoon vegetable oil
1 cup chopped onion
1 clove garlic, finely chopped
2 tablespoons tomato paste
1 1/2 tablespoons sweet Hungarian paprika
1 cup rich homemade chicken broth
1 cup dairy sour cream
1 tablespoon chopped fresh parsley

Rinse chicken pieces with cold running water and pat dry with paper towels. Sprinkle with salt and pepper. Sauté chicken in butter and oil in 10-inch skillet over medium heat until golden, 6 to 8 minutes on each side. Remove chicken from skillet and drain off all but 1 tablespoon of fat.

Sauté onion and garlic in fat over medium heat until light brown, about 6 minutes. Stir in tomato paste and

RIGHT: *For Satsivi, fillets of fresh fish are baked and served with a fragrant walnut sauce.*
OVERLEAF: *Rich sour cream is stirred into the tomato-based sauce of the classic* Chicken Paprika.

paprika until onion is evenly coated, then stir in broth. Return chicken to skillet and reduce heat to low. Simmer, covered, until chicken is done, 30 to 35 minutes.

Remove chicken from skillet and keep warm. Boil liquid in pan, stirring constantly, until slightly reduced and thickened, about 5 minutes. Stir in sour cream over low heat. Return chicken to skillet and heat just until chicken is hot, about 3 to 5 minutes. Transfer chicken to heated serving platter. Spoon any sauce remaining in skillet over chicken and sprinkle with parsley. Serve immediately.

PIEROGI

Filled "Pockets"
3½ DOZEN

2　cups all-purpose flour
2½　teaspoons salt
2　eggs
　　Cabbage, Cheese, or Meat and
　　　Mushroom Filling (recipes follow)

TO SERVE:

3　tablespoons butter, melted
3　tablespoons fine dry bread crumbs

Measure flour into mound on large wooden board. Make well in center and add ½ teaspoon of the salt, eggs and 3 tablespoons cold water. Beat with fork. Continue beating eggs in circular motion to incorporate flour gradually into egg mixture, using one hand to support flour on sides of well. When eggs are no longer runny, use fingers to continue mixing, adding more water as necessary to form dough that is soft but not sticky.

Knead dough on lightly floured surface until smooth, 8 to 10 minutes. Pat into flattened ball, cover with bowl and let stand 10 minutes.

Divide dough in half and cover 1 half with plastic wrap. Roll out other half as thin as possible and cut out circles of dough using 3-inch biscuit cutter. Place 1 level teaspoon of desired filling near center of each circle, brush edges lightly with water and fold circle over filling and pinch edges together to seal well. Repeat procedure to use remaining half of dough and filling. (Reroll and cut out scraps of dough.)

Heat 3 quarts water and remaining salt to boiling in 5-quart Dutch oven. Cook pierogi, about a dozen at a time, in boiling water until they rise to top, 1½ to 2½ minutes. Remove pierogi with slotted spoon and drain. Drizzle with melted butter and sprinkle with bread crumbs.

CABBAGE FILLING

½　pound cabbage, cut into thin wedges
3　tablespoons finely chopped onion

1   tablespoon butter
1/8 pound fresh mushrooms, cleaned and
     finely chopped
1/4 teaspoon salt
1/4 teaspoon caraway seeds
     Pinch freshly ground black pepper

Cook cabbage in ½ cup water in 2-quart covered saucepan over medium-high heat until tender, about 15 minutes. Drain and chop finely.

Sauté onion in butter in large skillet over medium heat until soft, about 3 minutes. Add cabbage, mushrooms and seasonings and cook 5 minutes, stirring frequently. Cool filling slightly before filling pierogi.

CHEESE FILLING

3/4 cup small-curd cottage cheese, drained
2   tablespoons raisins
1   egg yolk
1½   teaspoons sugar
1½   teaspoons butter, melted
1/4 teaspoon lemon juice

Press drained cottage cheese through sieve into bowl and blend in remaining ingredients.

MEAT AND MUSHROOM FILLING

2   tablespoons imported dried European
     mushrooms
1   cup boneless cooked meat, chopped
3   tablespoons finely chopped onion
1   tablespoon bacon drippings
1/8 teaspoon salt
     Pinch freshly ground black pepper
2   tablespoons dairy sour cream (optional)

Soak mushrooms in 1 cup boiling water until almost soft, about 1 hour. Drain and chop coarsely. Run cooked meat through food grinder with mushrooms or process about 5 seconds in food processor fitted with steel blade.

Sauté onion in bacon drippings in 10-inch skillet over medium heat until soft, about 5 minutes. Stir in meat mixture, salt and pepper and cook 5 minutes, stirring frequently. Remove from heat and stir in sour cream if desired. Cool slightly before filling pierogi.

GHIVETCH

Rumanian Mixed Vegetables
10 TO 12 SERVINGS

1/3 cup all-purpose flour
2½   teaspoons salt
3/4 teaspoon freshly ground black pepper
2   pounds boneless veal, cut into 1-inch
     cubes
2½   tablespoons butter

1/4 cup olive oil
2   medium onions, sliced
3   cloves garlic, finely chopped
1   cup rich homemade beef broth
1   cup dry red wine
3   tablespoons finely chopped fresh parsley

2   tablespoons tomato paste
2   carrots, pared and sliced
2   medium tomatoes, peeled, seeded and
         coarsely chopped
1   small green pepper, seeded and cut into
         ¼-inch strips
1   small eggplant, cut into ½-inch cubes
1   medium zucchini, cut into ½-inch cubes
1   leek, cleaned and thinly sliced
1   turnip, pared and chopped
1   celery root, pared and chopped
1   parsnip, pared and chopped
½   small head cabbage (about 12 ounces),
         thinly sliced
1   cup string beans, trimmed and
         julienned
½   cup seedless green grapes
½   teaspoon dried marjoram, crumbled
½   teaspoon dried thyme, crumbled

FOR GARNISH:

    Plain yogurt or dairy sour cream

Combine flour, ½ teaspoon of the salt and ¼ teaspoon of the pepper in large plastic bag. Add veal and toss until cubes are completely coated. Remove from flour with slotted spoon, shake off excess. Sauté veal in butter and oil in 5-quart Dutch oven over medium-high heat, stirring frequently, until brown on all sides, about 10 minutes.

Add onions and garlic and cook, stirring frequently, until onions are soft, about 5 minutes. Add all remaining ingredients except yogurt and stir until well mixed. Cook, covered, over high heat until liquid boils.

Place in preheated 350°F. oven. Bake, stirring several times during cooking, until vegetables are tender, about 1 hour. Serve hot. Garnish each serving with yogurt or sour cream.

BIGOS

Hunter's Stew

6 SERVINGS

4   large imported dried European
         mushrooms
½   pound cabbage, shredded
1   teaspoon salt
1   pound fresh sauerkraut
¼   pound bacon, diced
1   pound lean boneless beef, cut into 1-inch
         cubes
½   pound lean boneless pork, cut into
         1-inch cubes
½   pound lean boneless lamb, cut into
         1-inch cubes

1   cup chopped onion
1   cup chopped tart apple
2   medium tomatoes, peeled, seeded and
         chopped
1   cup rich homemade beef broth
½   cup dry red wine
¼   teaspoon ground allspice
¼   teaspoon freshly ground black pepper
½   pound kielbasa, cut into 1-inch slices

Soak mushrooms in 1 cup boiling water until soft, about 2 hours. Drain,

Bigos *is a hearty Polish stew that calls for beef, pork, lamb and* kielbasa.

reserving liquid, and cut into thin slices.

Meanwhile, place cabbage in colander and sprinkle with salt. Let stand 1 hour. Squeeze excess liquid out.

Rinse sauerkraut under cold running water, place in large bowl and cover with cold water. Let stand 15 minutes. Drain and squeeze out excess liquid.

Cook bacon in 5-quart Dutch oven over medium heat until crisp, stirring frequently. Remove with slotted spoon and reserve. Cook meats in bacon drippings, stirring frequently, until no longer red, about 10 minutes.

Set aside 1½ tablespoons of the bacon. Add remainder to meat, along with reserved mushrooms, cabbage, sauerkraut, onion, apple and tomatoes. Cook 10 minutes, stirring frequently. Add broth, wine, reserved mushroom liquid, allspice and pepper. Reduce heat to low. Cover and simmer until meat is almost tender, about 1 hour.

Add kielbasa and simmer, covered, 30 minutes longer. Transfer stew to heated serving dish and sprinkle with reserved bacon. Serve hot.

APFELSTRUDEL

Apple Strudel
15 TO 18 SERVINGS

1   egg
½   teaspoon salt
½   teaspoon vinegar
1¼ cups bread flour, plus additional ¼ cup
       as needed
       Apple Filling (recipe follows)
6   tablespoons butter, melted
½   cup fine dry bread crumbs
3   tablespoons sugar or fine dry bread
       crumbs

Combine ⅓ cup warm water (110° to 115°F.), egg, salt and vinegar in small mixing bowl. Beat until frothy. Beat in ½ cup flour. Stir in enough remaining flour to make a moderately stiff dough. Shape dough into smooth ball.

Knead dough on lightly floured surface until smooth, about 10 minutes. Cover dough with bowl and let stand 30 to 45 minutes.

Meanwhile, prepare Apple Filling and set aside.

Cover a 4 × 3-foot table or work surface with clean cloth and sprinkle with flour. Roll out dough on floured cloth as thinly as possible. Stretch dough by gently lifting under all edges with backs of hands until dough is paper-thin. Trim and discard any thick edges.

Brush dough with melted butter, covering completely. Sprinkle with bread crumbs. Spoon apple filling along long side, about 2 inches in fom edge, and sprinkle with nuts. Roll dough jelly-roll fashion and brush top with melted butter. Sprinkle evenly with sugar. Bend strudel into "U" shape or cut into several pieces and place on large greased baking sheet.

Bake in preheated 450°F. oven 10 minutes. Reduce heat to 400°F. and bake until strudel is crisp and golden brown, 25 to 30 minutes longer. Cool slightly on wire rack. Serve warm.

APPLE FILLING

$\frac{1}{3}$ cup sugar
$1\frac{1}{2}$ teaspoons ground cinnamon
4 cups peeled, cored and thinly sliced cooking apples (about $1\frac{1}{4}$ pounds)
$\frac{1}{4}$ cup golden raisins
2 tablespoons currants
$1\frac{1}{2}$ teaspoons grated lemon rind

Stir sugar and cinnamon together and sprinkle over apples in large mixing bowl. Add raisins, currants and lemon rind and mix until apples are completely coated.

NOTE: Traditionally, strudel dough is kneaded by lifting about 2 feet in the air and then slapping it against work surface. It also can be kneaded like bread dough, however.

Iberia

Spanish Comida (Midday Meal)

Gambas al Ajillo (Garlic Shrimp)
Gazpacho (Cold Vegetable Soup)
Lombo de Porco con Pimentos Vermelhos Doces
(Marinated Pork Chops with Sweet Red Peppers)
Escalibada (Mixed Grilled Vegetables)
Fresh Fruits and Cheeses
Espresso

RECOMMENDED WINES

Fumé Blanc
Grenache Rosé
Cabernet Sauvignon

Additional Spanish Recipes

Paella (Saffron Rice with Seafood and Chicken)
Huevos a la Flamenca (Baked Eggs with Vegetables and Meat)
Sopa de Ajo (Garlic Soup)
Churros Madrileños (Crisp Crullers)

Portuguese Recipes

Caldo Verde (Potato and Kale Soup)
Bolinhos de Bacalhau (Codfish Cakes)
Caldeirada (Fish Stew)
Carne de Porco a Alentejana (Marinated Pork)
Polla en Pepitoria (Chicken with Wine, Almonds and Garlic)

On a riverbank in southeastern Massachusetts, there is a rock inscribed with a legend that, translated, reads: "Miguel Cortereal by the will of God here chief of Indians 1511." Corte-Real, a young Portuguese nobleman, sailed west in 1502 to search, unsuccessfully, for his brother's lost expedition. He never returned, and it appears that he and his crew involuntarily became the first, albeit short-lived, European colony in New England. The rock is not far from New Bedford, which later became the "Portuguese Capital of America."

Fifty-four years after Cortereal's death, the Iberians made a more organized effort at colonization. King Philip of Spain dispatched Pedro Menendez de Aviles and 2,646 compatriots to establish a foothold in Florida. Menendez dug in with a will, attacking heretical French Lutheran settlers up and down the Atlantic coast and blazing trails in the Carolinas. He eventually sailed home to help Philip build an armada, but the Spaniards who remained etched their language, customs and Catholicism on the Southeast. Not long after, priests and expedition leaders brought the enduring mark of Spain to the Southwest as well.

After the glory days of sixteenth-century exploration, Portuguese and Spanish immigration to America became negligible. News of the California Gold Rush of 1849 rekindled the adventurous spirit of the Iberians, who began to come to the United States in greater numbers, but two factors combined to keep their profile low. First, both the Portuguese and the Spanish were regionalists rather than nationalists. The Portuguese divided themselves into three major groups—the Cape Verdeans, the Azoreans and the mainlanders—with even stronger local loyalties within each. Emi-

Striking a charismatic pose, this Basque sheepherder resembles a nineteenth-century American cowboy.

grants from Spain regarded themselves primarily as representatives of their province—for example, as Catalonians.

Secondly, while roughly 131,000 Spaniards and 221,000 Portuguese arrived in America between 1851 and 1920, their presence was eclipsed by the millions pouring in from other European countries. Small numbers, divided among many local loyalties, meant that Iberians rarely shaped much of America with the same force as larger, nationalistic groups.

The Basques, a people who trace their roots to Paleolithic times, proved an exception. Like most Iberians in the nineteenth century, they found themselves supporting too many people on too little land. Basque sailors, stirred by tales of gold, led the way to the American West in the 1850s. One captain left his ship in San Francisco, hunted for nuggets in Nevada, acquired an interest in some sheep and quickly made thousands of dollars in livestock. When news of opportunity in the sheep industry reached Spain, thousands of Basques traveled to Nevada, Oregon and southwest Idaho, turning Boise into the "Basque Capital." They lived a distinctively Basque life, speaking their own language, building *pelota* (handball) courts and adhering to their ancient traditions of unified families, hard work and democracy. Unlike most immigrants, the Basques met with more acceptance than alarm.

By 1878, a tropical chapter in immigration had begun: 114 Madeirans arrived in Hawaii, under contract to work the cane fields. Within ten years, the Portuguese population in Hawaii swelled to 12,000. While 8,000 or so Spaniards followed on their heels, nearly all of them moved on to California, and ultimately it was the Portuguese who influenced the look and sound of Hawaii. They created a semblance of Funchal, Madeira's capital, on the volcanic slopes of Honolulu and popularized the *braguinha*, a four-string

guitar. King Kalakaua's enchanted response to *braguinhas* prompt-
ed three Madeirans to manufacture them; before long, the islands
and the continental United States thrummed to the strains of what
was known in Hawaii as the "jumping flea," the ukulele.

On the mainland, the Iberians settled in a rough U shape
around the East, South and West. The Portuguese came to work
in New England factories, particularly the cotton mills of New
Bedford and Fall River, Massachusetts. Spaniards found jobs in
Philadelphia, Newark and New York; Spanish coal miners re-
created a Spanish community in West Virginia. Asturians from
northern Spain manufactured cigars in Tampa, Florida, while
other Spaniards were drawn to centuries-old colonial bastions
in Louisiana and California. Portuguese fishermen and farmers
sought economic betterment from San Diego to Sacramento.

*During idle hours, Basque musicians play
traditional folk songs.*

Many of the Portuguese who arrived in America around the turn
of the century were teenage boys fleeing military conscription.
Since it was illegal for males over fourteen to leave without paying
a huge deposit, they stowed away after their parents had paid their
passage and a little something to the steamship agent. Lawrence
Oliver, smuggled aboard in 1903, spent his sixteenth birthday
lurking behind a pier, waiting for a launch to take him to a White
Star steamer. Once he landed in America, he headed for "home"
in New Bedford; as one resident commented, a Portuguese would
neither "stop nor rest until he made a jaunt to this city." Lawrence swept floors in a cotton mill for $3.50 a week. In 1906 he
moved to California, believing that if he worked hard, he could
"achieve more than I could ever dream of acquiring in the
Azores." He went on to become a tuna millionaire in the state first
charted by Joao Cabrilho, a Portuguese, in 1542.

As Portuguese stowaways filled the cargos of U.S.-bound ships, record numbers of Spanish men traveled to America. Most were literate, skilled and headed for the industrial cities of the Northeast. It seems likely that many, in the transient tradition of their ancestors, came to make money rather than settle, since more than half eventually returned to Spain.

The Portuguese arrived in greater numbers and put down deeper roots. Though the image of fishermen in gaily painted boats tends to overshadow that of bean growers, the majority of Portuguese immigrants were unskilled, illiterate peasants hoping one day to own farms. The land deprivation they had known at home turned to their advantage on American soil. A saying arose in New England, where the Portuguese coaxed neglected soil into lush productivity: "A potato will not grow unless you speak to it in Portuguese." Azoreans, honing home-grown skills, soon dominated California's dairy industry.

Spanish and Portuguese paths in America did not often run parallel, yet, as Iberians, they shared beliefs and tastes. They were devout Roman Catholics. They loved and understood wine: Spanish priests planted the first vineyards in California, and one of the most trying adjustments for Portuguese immigrants, from a land famed for port and madeira, was getting by on beer. Iberians reproduced the strongly spiced sausages known as *chorizo* in America; they savored garlic soup, onions, peppers and saffron, and both the Basques and the Portuguese delighted in codfish preserved in salt. The Portuguese alone invented at least 365 ways to prepare cod.

Beyond this, both groups of Iberians shared much of the earliest history of America. The Spaniards, usually characterized as plunderers rather than settlers, introduced to the New World horses, cattle, goats, pigs, domestic poultry and sheep; oranges, lemons, limes, apricots, pears, apples and peaches; wheels and irrigation. They left lasting imprints on America's architecture, language and place names (including those of Florida, Colorado, Nevada and California) and created an American folk hero, the cowboy.

Portuguese explorers, perhaps the world's most daring navigators, were not only the first Europeans to set foot in New England and California, but they were also the first Europeans in North America to win a reputation for hospitality. When the Portuguese captaincy of Newfoundland, vested in the ill-fated Corte Real family, was ended in 1583, Sir Humfrey Gilbert arrived to claim the land for England. He found the Portuguese fishermen living there remarkably kind and wrote that when he left they "put aboarde our provision, which was wines, bread or ruske, fish, wette and drie, sweet oyles, besides many other. . . . In brief, wee were supplied of our wants commodiously, as if we had been in countrey or some citie populous and plenty of all things."

Proud representatives of one Iberian culture, these traditionally dressed Basque women celebrate in Boise, Idaho.

GAMBAS AL AJILLO

Garlic Shrimp
6 SERVINGS

2 to 4 cloves garlic, peeled and thinly
   sliced
1/2 teaspoon dried red pepper flakes
1 bay leaf
1/3 cup olive oil
3/4 pound small to medium shrimp, shelled
   and deveined
2 tablespoons fresh lemon juice
1 to 2 tablespoons chopped fresh parsley

Cook garlic with pepper and bay leaf in oil in large shallow skillet over medium-high heat until garlic is golden, 3 to 4 minutes. Add shrimp and cook just until they turn pink, 2 to 4 minutes. Do not overcook. Remove bay leaf. Transfer to serving dish, sprinkle with lemon juice and parsley and serve immediately.

GAZPACHO

Cold Vegetable Soup
6 TO 8 SERVINGS

1 1/2 pounds tomatoes, peeled and seeded
1 medium cucumber, cut into chunks
1 medium onion, cut into chunks
1 medium green pepper, seeded and cut
   into chunks
1 clove garlic, peeled and halved
2 cups tomato juice
1/4 cup red wine vinegar
1 to 2 tablespoons olive oil

FOR GARNISH:

1 cup French or Italian bread croutons
1 small onion, finely chopped
1/2 cucumber, pared and finely chopped
1/2 green pepper, finely chopped

Combine first eight ingredients in blender container or food processor bowl fitted with steel blade. Blend or process until finely chopped but not completely smooth, 30 to 60 seconds. Refrigerate until thoroughly chilled, 2 to 3 hours.

Stir soup and ladle into chilled bowls. Pass small bowls of croutons, chopped onion, cucumber and green pepper separately as garnishes.

RIGHT: *Ripe summer vegetables and olive oil are key ingredients in* Gazpacho.
OVERLEAF: *Sprinkled with parsley,* Garlic Shrimp *are perfectly matched with a crisp Fumé Blanc.*

LOMBO DE PORCO CON PIMENTOS VERMELHOS DOCES

Marinated Pork Chops
with Sweet Red Peppers

6 SERVINGS

3   large cloves garlic, peeled
½   teaspoon salt
½   teaspoon freshly ground black pepper
2   teaspoons olive oil
6   loin pork chops or pork loin slices, about
      ½-inch thick
2   tablespoons lard, oil or fat from pork
      trimmings

4   red peppers, seeded and cut into ¼-inch
      strips or 3 4-ounce jars whole pimen-
      tos, drained and cut
½   cup dry white wine
½   cup rich homemade chicken broth
1   to 2 teaspoons finely shredded lemon
      rind

Slender strands of lemon rind cover Lombo de Porco con Pimentos Vermelhos Doces,
served on a Portuguese platter from the 1820s.

Drop garlic cloves into blender container with motor running and add salt, pepper and oil. Blend until garlic is finely chopped. Place pork in single layer on covered with waxed paper and spread garlic mixture over both sides of pork. Cover with more waxed paper and marinate overnight in refrigerator or 2 to 3 hours at room temperature.

Melt lard in large skillet over medium-high heat, add chops and cook until deeply golden, 4 to 6 minutes on each side. Remove from skillet, add pepper strips to drippings and sauté until almost tender, about 5 minutes. Remove peppers from skillet and pour off any remaining fat.

Add wine and broth to skillet. Bring to boil, stirring to remove any crusty bits from bottom of skillet. Return pork and peppers to skillet. Re-

duce heat to low, cover and simmer until pork is tender, 15 to 20 minutes. Transfer pork and peppers to heated serving platter and keep warm in 200°F. oven. Boil liquid remaining in pan over high heat, stirring frequently, until reduced to about ¾ cup. Spoon over pork and peppers. Sprinkle with lemon rind. Serve hot.

ESCALIBADA

Mixed Grilled Vegetables
4 TO 6 SERVINGS

2   red peppers or 1 red and 1 green pepper
1   medium eggplant (about 1½ pounds)
3   or 4 medium onions
    Olive oil
    Salt
    Freshly ground black pepper

Place vegetables directly on oven rack, 2 to 4 inches from broiler, or on charcoal grill directly over hot coals. Cook, turning occasionally, until

flesh is tender and skin begins to char on all sides, about 30 minutes.

Place peppers in plastic bag to loosen skins. Peel eggplant and cut into ½-inch slices. Peel onions and cut into ½-inch slices. Peel and seed peppers and cut into ½-inch strips. Arrange vegetables on heated serving platter, drizzle with oil and season to taste with salt and pepper. Serve hot.

PAELLA

Saffron Rice with Seafood and Chicken
10 TO 12 SERVINGS

8   to 10 small lobster tails or langostinos,
    thawed if frozen
12 small clams in shells, scrubbed, or 12
    snails in shells
1   broiler-fryer chicken (2 to 2½ pounds),
    cut into serving pieces
½   cup olive oil
12 medium shrimp, shelled and deveined
½   pound chorizo or garlic-seasoned
    smoked pork sausage, cooked and
    sliced ¼ inch thick
1   pound lean boneless pork or ¾ pound
    pork plus ¼ pound ham, cut into
    ½-inch cubes
1   green pepper, seeded and diced
1   red pepper, seeded and diced
1   large tomato, peeled, seeded and diced
1   large onion, diced
2   cloves garlic, minced
3   cups uncooked short-grain Spanish or
    Italian Arborio rice
¼   teaspoon powdered saffron
4   cups rich homemade chicken broth
12 mussels, well-scrubbed
½   cup fresh or frozen peas

FOR GARNISH:

2 or 3 lemons, quartered

Cut ends from lobster tails with cleaver or chef's knife and chop each tail into 3 or 4 chunks. Place clams and 1 cup water in 3-quart saucepan. Cover and bring to boil over medium-high heat. Reduce heat to low and simmer until shells open, 5 to 7 min-utes. Remove from heat.

Sauté chicken pieces in ¼ cup oil in large skillet over medium-high heat until browned on all sides, about 15 minutes. Remove chicken from skillet.

Add lobster to skillet. Cook, stir-ring constantly, until shells turn pink, about 5 minutes. Remove from skil-let. Add shrimp and cook just until ends begin to curl, about 3 minutes. Remove from skillet. Add sausage and cook until lightly browned, 2 to 3 minutes on each side. Remove from skillet.

Add pork and remaining oil to skil-let and cook over medium-high heat, stirring constantly, until no longer pink, 8 to 10 minutes. Add peppers, tomato, onion and garlic and cook un-til liquid is completely evaporated, about 15 minutes. (At this point all prepared ingredients can be covered and refrigerated until 30 to 45 min-utes before serving time.)

Combine pork-vegetable mixture, rice and saffron in paella pan or very large skillet and stir to mix completely.

Drain liquid from clams into 2-cup measure and add water to equal 2 cups liquid. Pour liquid and chicken broth into 2-quart saucepan and bring to boil over high heat. Add boiling liquid to rice mixture in paella pan, place pan over high heat and bring to boil. Stir mixture well and remove from heat.

Tuck chicken pieces and mussels into rice mixture and arrange lobster, shrimp, sausage and clams over rice. Sprinkle with peas. Carefully place paella pan in preheated 400°F. oven and bake, uncovered, until rice is cooked and has absorbed all liquid, 25 to 30 minutes. Do not stir.

Remove pan from oven, cover loosely with foil and let stand 10 minutes. Uncover, garnish with lemon quarters and serve immediately, directly from pan.

To cook paella over charcoal on outdoor grill: Prepare paella as directed above but do not bake. Adjust grill height to 3 inches above coals. Ignite enough coals to make compact layer several inches larger in diameter than paella pan. Let coals burn until completely covered with ash and very hot. Put grill in place and set paella pan on grill. Cook, uncovered, until liquid is absorbed and rice is tender, about 20 minutes. Remove pan from grill, cover loosely with foil and let stand 10 minutes. Serve paella directly from pan. (Rice may form a crisp crust on bottom of pan; many consider this desirable.)

HUEVOS A LA FLAMENCA

Baked Eggs with Vegetables and Meat

6 SERVINGS

¼ pound chorizo or garlic-seasoned smoked pork sausage, cooked and thinly sliced
1 medium onion, chopped
1 red pepper, seeded and chopped
1 clove garlic, minced
¼ cup olive oil
¼ pound ham, diced
2 tablespoons chopped fresh parsley
1 bay leaf
6 eggs
12 asparagus tips, cooked until almost tender
½ cup fresh or frozen peas
   Pimiento strips

Brown chorizo on both sides in large skillet over medium heat, about 5 minutes. Drain and reserve. Wipe skillet clean with paper towels. Sauté onion, pepper and garlic in oil in skillet over medium-high heat, stirring frequently, until tender, 5 to 7 minutes. Add ham, chorizo, ¼ cup water, 1 tablespoon parsley and bay leaf. Bring to boil. Boil until almost all liquid has evaporated, about 15 minutes. Remove bay leaf.

Spread vegetable-meat mixture evenly in well-greased shallow 1½- or 2-quart casserole or baking dish. Make 6 indentations in mixture with

OVERLEAF: *Seafood and chicken served on a bed of saffron rice,* Paella *is a favorite Iberian dish.*

back of large spoon and break egg into each indentation. Arrange asparagus tips around eggs, sprinkle with peas and top with pimiento strips in decorative pattern. Cover tightly and bake in preheated 375°F. oven just until whites of eggs are set, 12 to 15 minutes. Uncover and sprinkle with remaining parsley. Serve hot from casserole.

SOPA DE AJO

Garlic Soup
6 TO 8 SERVINGS

1/4   *cup olive oil*
4   *cloves garlic, peeled and bruised with side of knife*
6   *slices French bread (1½ inches thick)*
6   *cups rich homemade chicken or beef broth*
1   *teaspoon paprika*
    Salt
    Freshly ground black pepper
2   *eggs, beaten*
2   *tablespoons chopped fresh parsley*

Cook garlic in oil in shallow casserole or large skillet over medium heat, stirring occasionally, until tender and golden, 3 to 5 minutes. Remove garlic. Add bread slices to oil, reduce heat to low and cook until golden on both sides, 2 to 3 minutes. Remove from casserole and reserve.

Mash garlic in small bowl with fork and add to casserole with broth, paprika and salt and pepper to taste. Bring to boil over medium-high heat, then remove from heat.

Arrange bread slices in single layer over broth in casserole and carefully pour beaten eggs over bread. Broil 3 to 4 inches from heat until golden, 3 to 5 minutes. Sprinkle with parsley and serve hot, directly from casserole.

CHURROS MADRILEÑOS

Crisp Crullers
2½ DOZEN

1   *tablespoon vegetable oil plus extra for frying*
½   *teaspoon salt*
2   *cups all-purpose flour*
    Powdered or granulated sugar

Bring 2 cups water, 1 tablespoon oil and salt to boil in 3-quart saucepan over high heat. Remove from heat and stir in flour all at once. Beat vigorously with wooden spoon until mixture forms a ball. (Dough will be *very* stiff.) Spread mixture out onto plate to cool until comfortable to handle.

Pour oil into 2- or 3-quart saucepan to depth of about 2 inches. Heat to 400°F.

Using star or ribbon disk, press dough through cookie press, directly into hot oil, cutting off strips about 6 inches long. Fry 4 or 5 strips at a time until richly browned on all sides, 5 to 7 minutes. Drain on paper towels. Sprinkle with sugar. Serve warm.

BOLINHOS DE BACALHAU

Codfish Cakes
5 OR 6 SERVINGS

2   *pounds salt cod fillets*
3   *cups coarse soft French or Italian bread crumbs*
¾   *cup olive oil*
2   *tablespoons minced fresh coriander (cilantro)*
2   *tablespoons minced fresh parsley*
1   *teaspoon minced fresh mint*
2   *tablespoons paprika*
¼   *teaspoon freshly ground black pepper*
1   *clove garlic, halved*

TO SERVE:

10 to 12 poached eggs
10 to 12 fresh parsley sprigs

Place cod in deep glass or stainless steel bowl. Cover with cold water, refrigerate 12 to 24 hours, changing water several times and rinsing fish with cold water between changes.

Rinse cod in cold water. Place in 3-quart saucepan and cover with cold water. Bring to boil over medium-high heat. Reduce heat to low and simmer until fish flakes easily with fork, about 20 minutes. Drain.

Combine bread crumbs and ½ cup oil in large bowl. Add coriander, parsley, mint, paprika and pepper and mix well. Remove any skin and bones from cod and flake flesh into crumb mixture. Beat with wooden spoon or process briefly in food processor fitted with steel blade, a third at a time, until mixture binds together. Using large spoon, ice cream scoop or ½-cup measuring cup, divide mixture into 10 to 12 equal portions. Shape into patties, each ½ to ¾ inch thick.

Sauté garlic in remaining ¼ cup oil in large skillet over medium heat until golden, 2 to 3 minutes. Remove and discard garlic. Place patties in skillet and sauté, 5 or 6 at a time, until deeply golden, about 5 minutes on each side. Keep cooked cakes warm on ovenproof platter in preheated 200°F. oven while cooking remaining patties. To serve, top each codfish cake with poached egg and garnish with parsley. Serve hot.

CALDO VERDE

Potato and Kale Soup
6 SERVINGS

¼ pound linguiça, chorizo or garlic-
    seasoned smoked pork sausage
4 medium potatoes (about 1½ pounds),
    pared and cut into ¼-inch cubes
¼ cup olive oil
½ teaspoon salt
¼ teaspoon freshly ground black pepper
1 pound fresh kale or collard greens

Heat 6 cups water in 4- or 5-quart saucepan over medium-high heat just until simmering. Add sausage and simmer 10 minutes. Remove sausage, drain and cut into thin slices. Return water to boil over medium heat. Add potatoes and cook until soft, 10 to 15 minutes. Remove from heat. Mash potatoes in liquid in pan.

Add oil, salt and pepper.

Rinse kale thoroughly under cold running water, remove stems and any bruised leaves. Drain in colander. Tightly roll up handful of leaves and cut into fine shreds, then repeat until all kale is shredded. (Rolls of kale leaves can also be shredded by inserting into food processor feed tube fitted with medium slicing blade.) Add kale to potatoes in pan. Bring to boil over medium-high heat, stirring frequently. Boil 5 minutes. Add sausage slices and boil 1 minute longer. Ladle into individual soup bowls, dividing sausage slices evenly between bowls.

CALDEIRADA

Fish Stew
8 SERVINGS

24 small clams, well scrubbed
½ cup olive oil
3 medium tomatoes, peeled, seeded and
    chopped
2 medium onions, chopped
2 medium potatoes, pared and cut into
    ½-inch cubes
1 green pepper, seeded and chopped
1 leek, cleaned and thinly sliced
1 large carrot, pared and chopped
2 cloves garlic, minced
3 tablespoons chopped fresh parsley

1 teaspoon salt
¼ teaspoon freshly ground black pepper
2 pounds assorted fresh fish fillets or
    steaks (halibut, haddock, cod, red
    snapper, flounder or other saltwater
    fish), skin removed, cut into 1½-inch
    chunks
1 pound squid, thawed if frozen
    (optional)
½ lemon, thinly sliced
1 cup dry white wine
6 slices (each 1 inch thick) French or

Italian bread
1 *clove garlic, halved*

Place clams in 6- to 8-quart stockpot and pour in ¼ cup of the oil. Combine tomatoes, onions, potatoes, green pepper, leek, carrot, garlic, 2 tablespoons parsley, salt and pepper in large bowl and toss to mix thoroughly. Spoon half mixture over clams and top with fish chunks.

If using squid, rinse well under cold running water and remove and discard ink sacs. Cut off tentacles and cut each into 2 to 3 pieces. Discard viscera and eye sections. Remove cartilage from inside tail sections and discard. Cut tails crosswise into ½-inch slices and cut each fin in half.

Sprinkle squid pieces over fish. Top with remaining vegetable mixture and lemon slices. Pour wine and 1 cup water over all. Cover and bring to boil over high heat. Reduce heat to low and simmer until clams open and fish flakes easily with fork, 15 to 20 minutes.

Rub bread slices on both sides with cut garlic. Sauté in remaining oil in large skillet over medium-low heat until golden, 2 to 3 minutes each side. Drain on paper towels.

To serve, place bread slice in each serving bowl and ladle caldeirada over. Sprinkle with remaining parsley. Serve immediately.

CARNE·DE PORCO A ALENTEJANA

Marinated Pork
4 TO 6 SERVINGS

1 *cup dry white wine*
1 *teaspoon paprika*
2 *cloves garlic, crushed*
1 *bay leaf*
2 *pounds lean boneless pork, cut into 1-inch cubes*
¼ *cup olive oil*

TO SERVE:

Hot cooked rice
12 *small to medium clams, steamed and shucked*

Combine wine, paprika, garlic and bay leaf in deep glass or stainless steel bowl. Add pork cubes and stir to mix. Cover and refrigerate several hours or overnight, stirring occasionally.

Remove pork from marinade and drain well, reserving marinade. Pat dry with paper towels. Cook pork in oil in large skillet over medium heat, stirring frequently, until no longer pink, 8 to 10 minutes. Add ½ cup marinade and cover skillet tightly.

OVERLEAF: Caldo Verde *is served in a Portuguese hand-decorated tureen from the 1820s.*

Reduce heat to low and simmer until pork is very tender, about 20 minutes. Uncover and simmer until pan juices are slightly reduced, about 10 minutes. Serve pork on hot rice, topped with clams.

POLLO EN PEPITORIA

Chicken with Wine, Almonds and Garlic
4 TO 6 SERVINGS

1   broiler-fryer chicken (3 to 3½ pounds), cut into serving pieces
¼   cup olive oil
2   medium onions, chopped
1   cup dry white wine
3   tablespoons chopped fresh parsley
1   bay leaf
24   whole almonds, blanched
1   clove garlic
⅛   teaspoon powdered saffron
2   hard-cooked egg yolks

TO SERVE:

Hot cooked rice

Rinse chicken pieces with cold running water and pat dry with paper towels. Sauté in oil in large skillet over medium heat until browned on all sides, about 15 minutes. Remove from skillet and reserve. Remove all but 2 tablespoons drippings from skillet. Add onions and sauté until soft but not browned, about 5 minutes.

Return chicken to skillet. Add wine, 1 cup water, 2 tablespoons parsley and bay leaf. Reduce heat to low, cover and simmer until chicken is almost cooked, 15 to 20 minutes.

Pulverize almonds in blender or food processor. Add garlic and saffron and blend well. Add egg yolks and blend again. Add about ½ cup liquid from skillet and blend or process until smooth. Stir almond mixture into remaining liquid in skillet. Cover and simmer 10 minutes longer.

Transfer chicken from skillet to heated serving platter and cover with foil to keep hot. Boil liquid remaining in skillet over medium-high heat until reduced by half, about 10 minutes. Remove bay leaf. Pour over chicken and sprinkle with remaining parsley. Serve hot with rice.

A selection of Spanish cheeses rests on an eighteenth-century Portuguese cloth.

Jewish

Sabbath Menu

Gefülte Fish with Chrain
Chicken Soup with Mandlen (Soup Nuts)
Cholent
Challah (Braided Egg Bread)
Tomato and Cucumber Salad
Kugel (Noodle Pudding)

RECOMMENDED WINES

Fumé Blanc
Merlot

Additional Recipes

Latkes (Potato Pancakes)
Tsimmes (Fruited Stew)
Lekach (Honey Cake)
Borscht (Beet and Cabbage Soup)
Kasha Varnishkes
Chopped Liver
Mandelbrot (Almond Bread Slices)
Blintzes (Cheese-Filled Pancakes)

The history of Jews in America began with an irony that would not be appreciated for centuries. On August 2, 1492, the door slammed shut on 700 years of cultural harmony and equality when Catholic Spain banished its Jews. One day later, Christopher Columbus, backed by the money and prayers of the Spanish monarchy, sailed off to find the place that would one day hold the world's largest Jewish population.

Jewish immigrants found civic and religious freedom in their new chosen land, America.

Some of the exiled found sanctuary in Brazil, but in 1654 the Portuguese expelled the Jews of Iberia, the Sephardim. One of the last ships to leave carried twenty-three Jews who were nearly intercepted by Spaniards near Jamaica. A French sea captain rescued them and, demanding an exorbitant price for his gallantry, took them to the Dutch colony of New Amsterdam, arriving in September just before Rosh Hashanah, the Jewish New Year.

Against the wishes of Peter Stuyvesant, the governor of New Amsterdam, the Dutch West India Company decided the Jews could settle. New Amsterdam had become New York by the time the Jews were allowed to build a synagogue, in 1728. They called their congregation Shearith Israel, "Remnant of Israel."

During the 1700s, Jews were drawn to America much as the Puritans had been—for its religious tolerance and economic opportunities. While most worked as merchants and artisans, some struck off in other directions, including a group of London Jews who erroneously decided in 1732 that Savannah, Georgia, was a fine location for visionary vintners. Several Jews, notably the financier Haym Salomon, participated in the Revolutionary War with distinction. Despite occasional flickers of anti-Semitism, the 3,000 Jews who lived in America by the end of the century were full-fledged citizens. George Washington, writing to a Hebrew congregation in 1790, expressed the hope that every one could "sit in safety under his own vine and fig-tree, and there shall be none to make him afraid."

Conditions were far less benevolent in Germany, where the Jewish population was oppressed with myriad taxes and degrading restrictions. Starting in the 1820s, emigration picked up momentum until entire communities were crossing the Atlantic together. Well-organized groups carried ceremonial objects; some even brought religious officials to oversee proper preparation of food during the journey. Eventually the Yiddish word *kosher*, describing food that meets the standards of Jewish dietary laws, became an Americanism for "genuine."

This second and much larger wave of Jewish immigrants were Ashkenazim, "Eastern" Jews. They pronounced Hebrew differently from the Sephardim and had never enjoyed the company of kings and noblemen in Europe, as the Sephardim could boast of having done. But the main difference between the American Sephardim and the immigrant German Ashkenazim in the 1800s was that the Sephardim had become natives: they spoke English and blended with their communities.

Most newly arrived German Jews turned to an occupation that required little or no initial investment and a minimum of English: peddling. Often, especially in the South, they were met with warm hospitality. They wandered from one isolated farm to another, bringing notions and, equally valuable, neighborhood news. Step by step, they worked their way up the trade ladder to the top rung of store owner, creating a vital, prosperous mercantile distribution network across the country.

By 1880, America's Jewish population had risen to 250,000. Reform Judaism, which streamlined traditional Judaism from 613 commandments to 8 principles, was taking hold. American Jews were finding ways to preserve their heritage even as they adapted to the West's open society. This theological modernization was barely in place when the third and largest wave of Jewish immigrants broke through the boundaries of the Russian Pale and flooded into America.

The Russian Pale formed a geographical prison for the vast majority of Eastern European Jews. Sealed off from the rest of the world, they lived in a bleak grind of hard labor and poverty, stripped of civil rights by the czarist regime. During the 1800s, the Pale's population exploded. So did anti-Semitism. In 1881 and 1882, pogroms—violent, government-condoned attacks—set off a desperate rush of emigration that slowed only when America's quota restrictions became law in 1924.

This chicken market at 55 Hester Street, shown in a 1937 photograph by Berenice Abbot, was in the heart of the largest Jewish community in America, Manhattan's Lower East Side.

The 2.3 million Jews who fled Eastern Europe settled primarily in the largest cities of the East and Midwest. Most stayed in New York, where the Lower East Side came to resemble Eastern Europe in miniature: a street of immigrants from Warsaw, another from Rumania. Yiddish, an Ashkenazic language written in the Hebrew alphabet, served as the common denominator. Hundreds of *landsmanshaften*, clubs made up of people from the same village, provided everything from housing, jobs and burial services to dances and banquets. These clubs also gave the immigrants a familiar context in foreign surroundings, a place where their personal history was known and appreciated.

Jewish immigrants from Eastern Europe pursued long-thwarted ambitions with tireless energy. If they could not make the leap from laborer to professional in their lifetime, they would make sure their children obtained that most treasured benefit, educa-

A visitor to today's Lower East Side will find many of the same flavors, smells and sounds as were offered in this kosher market fifty years ago.

tion. Some actually studied law or medicine while they learned English, but the majority were highly skilled craftsmen who hoped to move gradually beyond factory work. In 1900, the garment industry employed one out of three Russian Jews.

Pauline Newman, who came from Lithuania in 1901, began cutting threads at the Triangle Shirtwaist Company at the age of eight. "We started work at seven thirty in the morning, and during the busy season we worked until nine in the evening," she recalls. "They didn't pay you overtime and they didn't give you anything for supper money. Sometimes they'd give you a little apple pie if you worked late. That was all. Very generous." After the Triangle fire of 1911 that killed 145 workers, Pauline beame an organizer and finally educational director of the International Ladies Garment Workers Union.

Jewish tastes and dietary rules gave rise to new industries. Meat was slaughtered according to kosher laws; Jewish cakes and breads sprinkled with poppyseeds were baked year-round; commercial matzoh appeared at Passover; and pickles, smoked fish and pastrami were produced for delicatessens. The thirst for soda water, which the immigrants nicknamed "the worker's champagne," was so overpowering that by 1907 more than a hundred firms manufactured and sold it. Another thirst sprang up during Prohibition, when a suspicious number of converts to Judaism carried cards entitling them to buy sacramental kosher wine.

The fourth wave of Jewish immigration lasted from the 1930s until the Displaced Persons Act expired in 1952. From 1933 to 1943, 168,000 Jews came to America to escape the holocaust. Except for 1,000 German children who were immediately placed in private homes, the United States refused to relax the constricting immigration quotas of 1924. Even so, the Jewish immigrants of this period brought America a wealth of talent and intellect: musicians, scholars, architects, scientists. No fewer than twelve refugees, including Albert Einstein, won the Nobel Prize after arriving in the United States.

The Displaced Persons Act of 1948 was a limited gesture, but it allowed 63,000 more Jews into America. Having survived the unthinkable, those Jews flung themselves back into living: They married, built new families, learned English, savored the comfort of possessions. Ruth Gay, in *Jews in America*, tells the story of one Jew who expressed his hunger for the shelter and sustenance of America very precisely. He explained that he wanted an apartment, and in that apartment he wanted a basket of fresh fruit. During the war, fruit could only be dreamed about. Now, in America, a piece of fruit held the sweet taste of freedom.

Photographs like this one by Lewis W. Hine of Jewish immigrant families working in New York's infamous sweatshops spurred important reforms in the nation's child labor laws.

GEFÜLTE FISH

8 SERVINGS

5   to 6 pounds whole fresh fish (pike, white-fish, carp or bass)
4   large onions, peeled and sliced
4   carrots, pared and sliced
1   parsnip, pared and sliced
3   teaspoons sugar
2½ teaspoons salt
1   teaspoon freshly ground black pepper
2   large onions, peeled and quartered
2   carrots, pared and cut into 1-inch pieces
3   eggs
¼   cup matzoh meal

TO SERVE:

Chrain (recipe follows)

Clean, fillet and skin fish (or ask fish seller to do it). Reserve bones, heads and skin for stock. Remove and discard gills. Rinse all fish parts well in cold water.

Pack bones and trimmings in even layer into bottom of 6-quart or larger stock pot. Arrange sliced onions, sliced carrots and parsnip evenly over fish bones and trimmings. Add enough water to barely cover vegetables. Sprinkle with 2 teaspoons sugar, 1½ teaspoons salt and ½ teaspoon pepper. Bring to boil over high heat while preparing fish mixture. (If stock boils before fish mixture is ready, reduce temperature to low and simmer.)

Grind or finely chop together fish fillets, remaining onions, remaining carrots, eggs, matzoh meal, 2 tablespoons ice water, remaining salt, sugar and pepper. (If desired, all ingredients may be processed in food processor until smooth and well blended, 15 to 30 seconds. Work with small batches if work bowl is small.) Mixture should be thick enough to mound and to support a spoon standing upright. Adjust consistency, if necessary, by adding a small amount of additional ice water or matzoh meal.

Gently shape mixture into balls, dividing with well-rounded tablespoon or ¼-cup measure. Rinse hands and utensils frequently with cold water while shaping to prevent sticking.

Arrange balls in single layer over vegetables in simmering stock (if there are too many for a single layer, stack remaining balls over first layer). Cover pot tightly and simmer over low heat 1 hour. Uncover, taste stock and adjust seasonings if necessary. Cover and simmer 1 hour longer.

Remove from heat. Cool 30 minutes, then refrigerate until cold, 2 to 3 hours. Lift fish balls from stock with slotted spoon and arrange in deep serving platter or bowl. Lift out ½ to 1 cup each of the onion and carrot slices and spoon over fish. Cover tightly and refrigerate several hours or overnight.

Strain stock, discarding vegetables and fish parts. Pour into 9-inch square pan, cover and refrigerate until ready to serve (stock should jell).

To serve, cut jellied stock into ½-inch cubes and arrange around fish and vegetables on platter. Serve cold with *Chrain*.

CHRAIN

½   *cup freshly grated or prepared horse-*radish, *drained*
½   *cup shredded cooked beets*
2   *tablespoons sugar*
2   *tablespoons white vinegar*
½   *teaspoon salt*

Combine all ingredients in small saucepan and boil over high heat. Remove from heat and cool slightly. Taste and adjust seasoning, if necessary. Cover and refrigerate until ready to serve.

CHICKEN SOUP

4 TO 6 SERVINGS

1   *stewing chicken (2 to 3 pounds)*
4   *small to medium carrots, pared and cut into 1-inch pieces*
4   *stalks celery, cut into 1-inch pieces*
2   *small to medium onions, peeled and quartered*
1   *parsnip, pared and cut into 1-inch pieces*
3   *to 4 sprigs fresh parsley*
   Salt
   Freshly ground black pepper

TO SERVE:

Mandlen (recipe follows)

Cut chicken into quarters, discarding excess fat. (Reserve liver for another use.) Arrange chicken parts in single layer in 5-quart Dutch oven or 6-quart stockpot. Top with carrots, celery, onions, parsnip and parsley. Add enough water to cover chicken, about 2½ to 3 quarts. Bring to boil over high heat. Reduce heat to low, cover and simmer until chicken is tender, 2 to 3 hours.

Remove chicken and vegetables with slotted spoon and cool slightly. Remove chicken from bones and cut into bite-sized pieces. Skim off and discard fat from broth. Strain broth into large bowl. Return broth, chicken and vegetables to Dutch oven. Heat to simmering over medium-high heat. Season to taste with salt and pepper. Serve hot with *Mandlen*.

MANDLEN

Soup Nuts
2 CUPS

3   tablespoons chicken fat
½   teaspoon salt
1   cup matzoh meal
2   eggs

Bring ¼ cup water, chicken fat and salt to boil in medium saucepan over high heat. Remove from heat and stir in matzoh meal. Add eggs and beat well. Let mixture stand until cool enough to handle, 10 to 15 minutes.

Form into several ropes, each about ½ inch in diameter. Cut or pinch off ½-inch lengths of dough and roll each between palms to form balls.

Arrange balls on lightly oiled 15½ × 10½ × 1-inch jelly-roll pan. Bake in preheated 400°F. oven. Shake pan several times while baking to brown dough evenly. Bake until browned, about 20 minutes. Cool on pan. Store in tightly covered container until ready to use.

KUGEL

Noodle Pudding
12 SERVINGS

2   teaspoons salt
12   ounces wide egg noodles
6   eggs
1   cup large curd cream-style cottage cheese
1   cup milk
2   3-ounce packages cream cheese, softened
⅓   cup sugar
1   teaspoon vanilla extract
1   teaspoon ground cinnamon
½   teaspoon ground nutmeg
1   cup golden raisins
4   tablespoons butter, melted

Bring 1 gallon of water and salt to boil in 6-quart stockpot over high heat. Stir in noodles. Cook until tender, 6 to 7 minutes for dried, packaged noodles (4 to 5 minutes for homemade fresh noodles). Drain and place in large mixing bowl.

Beat eggs, cottage cheese, milk, cheese, sugar, vanilla and spices with electric mixer, blender or food processor until smooth. Add to noodles, add raisins and mix well. Pour into well-oiled 13 × 9 × 2-inch baking dish. Drizzle with melted butter.

Bake in preheated 325°F. oven until knife inserted off center comes out clean, 30 to 40 minutes. Cool on wire rack. Serve warm or cold.

Often better than medicine, Chicken Soup *is the Jewish cure-all.*

CHOLENT

6 SERVINGS

1 cup dry lima or Great Northern beans
1 tablespoon chicken or beef fat
3 pounds beef short ribs, cut into 2- to
  3-inch lengths and well trimmed
2 large onions, chopped
2 cloves garlic, finely chopped
4 medium carrots, pared and cut into
  2-inch lengths
2 tablespoons barley
1 teaspoon salt
½ teaspoon freshly ground black pepper

Wash and sort beans, discarding any that are discolored. Place in 1- or 2-quart saucepan. Add water to cover. Bring to boil over high heat. Remove from heat, cover and let stand 1 hour.

Heat fat in large stockpot or Dutch oven over medium-high heat until hot, about 2 minutes. Reduce heat to medium and add short ribs. Cook turning frequently, until browned on all sides, 15 to 20 minutes. Add onions and garlic. Cook, stirring frequently, until soft, 8 to 10 minutes.

Drain beans and add to Dutch oven with all remaining ingredients. Add just enough water to cover all ingredients. Cover tightly and place on bottom rack of oven. Bake at 250°F. until meat is tender and falls from bone, about 8 hours or overnight. Skim off and discard any fat. Transfer to large heated serving bowl. Serve hot.

CHALLAH

Braided Egg Bread

1 LOAF

2 tablespoons sugar
1 package active dry yeast (1 scant
  tablespoon)
½ cup milk
2 tablespoons butter
1 teaspoon salt
⅛ teaspoon powdered saffron
3 to 3½ cups all-purpose flour
2 eggs, slightly beaten
  Vegetable oil
1 tablespoon poppy or sesame seeds

Combine ¼ cup warm water (110° to 115°), sugar and yeast in large mixing bowl. Let stand until bubbly, about 5 minutes. Heat milk, butter, salt and saffron in small saucepan over low heat just until warm. Add to yeast mixture.

Beat 1½ cups flour into yeast mixture until smooth, about 2 minutes on medium speed of electric mixer or 300 strokes by hand. Measure 1½ tablespoons beaten egg into small bowl, cover with plastic wrap and re-

Long, slow cooking is the secret to Cholent.

serve. Beat remaining egg into flour mixture. Stir in enough additional flour to make moderately stiff dough.

Turn dough onto lightly floured surface. Knead until smooth and satiny, 8 to 10 minutes. Shape into ball and place in lightly greased bowl, turning to grease all sides. Cover and let rise in warm place (80° to 85°F.) until doubled in bulk, about 1½ hours.

Punch dough down. Cover and let rest 10 minutes. Divide into 3 equal parts. Shape each into rope about 20 inches long. Braid ropes loosely together on greased baking sheet. Tuck ends under and pinch to seal. Brush lightly with oil and let stand in warm place until almost doubled in bulk, 30 to 40 minutes.

Brush braid with reserved egg. Sprinkle with poppy seeds. Bake in preheated 375°F. oven until golden brown, 25 to 30 minutes. Transfer to wire rack and cool completely.

LEKACH

Honey Cake
1 CAKE

⅔ cup light brown sugar, firmly packed
⅔ cup honey
½ cup vegetable shortening
2 eggs
2½ cups all-purpose flour
1 teaspoon baking powder
1 teaspoon ground cinnamon
½ teaspoon salt
½ teaspoon baking soda
¼ cup strongly brewed coffee
½ cup currants
½ cup chopped almonds or walnuts
1 teaspoon grated orange rind

Beat brown sugar, honey and shortening together in large mixer bowl at high speed of electric mixer until light and fluffy, about 2 minutes. Add eggs, one at a time, beating well after each addition. Stir together flour, baking powder, cinnamon, salt and soda. Add to honey mixture alternately with coffee, beating well after each addition and ending with flour mixture. Stir in currants, nuts and orange rind. Pour batter into oiled 9 × 5 × 3-inch loaf pan.

Bake in preheated 350°F. oven until cake tester inserted in center comes out clean, 1 to 1¼ hours. Cool in pan on wire rack. To serve, turn cake out of pan and slice.

Challah, *which is served on special holy days, is wrapped in a nineteenth-century linen cover.*

LATKES

Potato Pancakes
6 TO 8 SERVINGS

6   medium potatoes (about 2 pounds), pared
1   small onion, grated
2   tablespoons chopped fresh parsley
2   eggs, beaten
1   teaspoon salt
1   teaspoon chopped fresh chives
1/4   teaspoon ground nutmeg
1/4   teaspoon freshly ground black pepper
2   tablespoons all-purpose flour
1/4   cup vegetable oil

TO SERVE:

Applesauce
Dairy sour cream

Shred potatoes and immerse in cold water to prevent discoloration. Combine onion, parsley, eggs, salt, chives, nutmeg and pepper in large mixing bowl. Drain potatoes and pat dry with paper towels. Add to onion mixture, sprinkle with flour and mix thoroughly.

Heat oil in 10-inch skillet over medium heat. Drop potato mixture by rounded tablespoonsful into oil. Cook until crisp and golden on bottom, about 5 minutes. Turn over and cook about 5 minutes longer. Serve hot with applesauce and sour cream.

TSIMMES

Fruited Stew
6 TO 8 SERVINGS

2   tablespoons chicken fat or vegetable oil
3   pounds lean beef brisket
2   medium to large onions, chopped
6   carrots, pared and sliced 1/2 inch thick
3   medium sweet potatoes (about 2 pounds), pared and sliced 1/2 inch thick
1/2   pound pitted prunes
1   teaspoon salt
1/2   teaspoon ground nutmeg
1/4   teaspoon freshly ground black pepper

Heat chicken fat in 5-quart Dutch oven or large electric skillet over medium-high heat about 1 minute. Add brisket and cook until browned, about 5 minutes on each side. Remove from pan. Add onions to pan drippings and sauté over medium heat until soft, about 5 minutes. Return brisket to pan and add just enough water to cover. Bring to boil over high heat. Reduce heat to medium-low. Cover and simmer until meat is barely tender, about 1½ hours.

Arrange carrots, sweet potatoes and

LEFT: Latkes, *the traditional Chanukah repast, are accompanied by sour cream and applesauce.*
OVERLEAF: Tsimmes—*the raw ingredients are combined to create a rich fruited stew.*

prunes over and around meat. Sprinkle with salt, nutmeg and pepper. Cover and simmer, until vegetables are very tender, about 2 hours longer.

Remove meat from pan and slice across grain. Arrange slices on heated serving platter. Spoon vegetables, prunes and pan juices over meat. Serve hot.

BORSCHT

Beet and Cabbage Soup

8 TO 10 SERVINGS

4   *pounds beef soup bones*
2   *pounds cabbage, shredded*
1   *pound beets (about 4 medium), pared*
     and sliced
2   *large onions, chopped*
1   *can (28 ounces) tomatoes*
¼ *cup brown sugar*
¼ *cup fresh lemon juice*
2   *teaspoons caraway seeds*

FOR GARNISH:

Dairy sour cream

Place bones in 5-quart Dutch oven or 6-quart stockpot. Add enough water to cover. Bring to boil over high heat. Skim off foam. Reduce heat to medium-low, cover and simmer 1½ hours.

Add cabbage, beets, onions and tomatoes. Cover and simmer until meat on bones is very tender, 1½ to 2 hours longer. Using slotted spoon, lift bones from soup and remove meat, discarding bones. Dice meat and return to soup. Skim fat off soup. Add brown sugar, lemon juice and caraway seeds. Simmer, uncovered, 30 minutes longer. Serve hot, topping each serving with a dollop of sour cream.

KASHA VARNISHKES

6 TO 8 SERVINGS

1   *cup medium-grind kasha (buckwheat*
     groats)
1   *egg, beaten*
¼ *pound bow-tie or small shell noodles*
1   *medium onion, finely chopped*
2   *tablespoons chicken fat*
½ *to 1 teaspoon salt*
¼ *to ½ teaspoon freshly ground black*
     pepper

Blend kasha and egg in 2-quart saucepan until kasha is completely coated. Cook over medium heat, stirring constantly to avoid scorching, until each grain is dry and separate, 2 to 3 minutes. Add 2 cups boiling water. Reduce heat to low, cover and cook until kasha is tender, 10 to 15 minutes.

Bring 2 quarts to boil in 4- or 5-quart saucepan over high heat. Stir in noodles. Cook until tender, 6 to 8 minutes. Drain.

Sauté onion in chicken fat in small skillet over medium heat until soft, about 5 minutes. Remove from heat.

Stir noodles, onion, salt and pepper into kasha. Transfer to heated serving bowl. Serve hot.

CHOPPED LIVER

2 CUPS

1   pound chicken livers
3   to 4 tablespoons chicken fat or vegetable oil
2   hard-cooked eggs, shelled
1   medium onion, finely chopped
1   to 1½ teaspoons salt
¼   teaspoon freshly ground black pepper
¼   teaspoon sugar, if desired

TO SERVE:

Lettuce leaves

Trim and discard any fat from livers. Cook livers in 3 tablespoons chicken fat in 10-inch skillet over medium heat, stirring frequently, until done, 10 to 12 minutes. Using slotted spoon, lift livers from skillet and cool slightly. Reserve drippings in skillet.

When livers are cool enough to handle, combine with hard-cooked eggs and chop or grind. Return to skillet, stir in onion and seasonings and mix. Add remaining chicken fat, if necessary.

Pack liver mixture into oiled bowl. Cover tightly and refrigerate several hours or overnight.

To serve, turn out of bowl onto lettuce-lined serving plate or scoop from bowl onto individual lettuce-lined serving plates.

NOTE: Ground liver has a finer texture and is best for molding. Hand-chopped liver is more crumbly and is better suited to scooping.

MANDELBROT

Almond Bread Slices
3 DOZEN

4   eggs
1   cup sugar
8   tablespoons butter, melted
1   tablespoon brandy or orange juice
1   teaspoon grated orange rind
1   teaspoon grated lemon rind
½   teaspoon almond extract
½   teaspoon vanilla extract
4   cups all-purpose flour
2   teaspoons baking powder

¼ teaspoon salt
1½ cups finely chopped blanched almonds

Beat eggs in large mixer bowl at high speed of electric mixer until thick and lemon-colored, about 5 minutes. Add sugar. Beat until sugar is dissolved and mixture forms a ribbon as it falls from beater, about 3 minutes. Fold in butter, brandy, orange and lemon rind, almond extracts and vanilla. Sift flour, baking powder and salt together. Gently stir into batter along with almonds.

Turn dough onto lightly floured surface and gently knead into a ball. Divide in half. Shape each half into a flattened roll about 15 inches long, 3 inches wide and 1½ inches thick.

Place rolls on oiled 15½ × 10½ × 1-inch jelly roll pan or large baking sheet.

Bake in preheated 350°F. oven until firm and lightly browned, about 35 minutes. Remove from oven. Increase oven temperature to 400°F. Carefully transfer each warm roll to cutting board. Cut diagonally into ½-inch slices. Arrange slices, cut side up on baking sheet, using second pan if necessary. Return to oven and bake just until slices begin to brown, about 5 minutes. Remove from oven, turn each slice over and bake 5 minutes longer. Cool on pan on wire rack. Store in tightly covered container.

BLINTZES

Cheese-Filled Pancakes
6 SERVINGS

2 eggs, beaten
1 cup milk
5 tablespoons butter, melted (plus extra for pan)
¼ teaspoon salt
⅔ cup all-purpose flour
   Cheese Filling (recipe follows)
3 tablespoons butter

TO SERVE:

   Dairy sour cream
   Blueberry or other fruit preserves, or applesauce

Blend together eggs, milk, 2 table-

spoons melted butter and salt in small mixing bowl. Measure flour into large mixing bowl. Add liquid mixture. Beat with whisk until smooth.

Heat 6-inch crepe or omelet pan over medium heat. Brush lightly with melted butter, pour in 2 tablespoons batter and rotate pan quickly so that batter covers bottom. Cook 1 minute, until slightly dry. Invert pancake, cooked side up, onto waxed paper. Repeat with remaining batter.

Spoon 1 rounded tablespoonful *Cheese Filling* onto center of each pancake. Fold edges over to cover completely.

Melt remaining 3 tablespoons butter in 10-inch skillet over medium heat. Cook filled pancakes in butter until filling is cooked through and outsides are lightly browned, 3 to 5 minutes, on each side. Serve hot with sour cream and preserves or apple sauce.

CHEESE FILLING

1	pound cottage cheese, drained and sieved
1	egg, beaten
2	tablespoons sugar
1/2	teaspoon ground cinnamon
1/2	teaspoon grated lemon rind
1/2	teaspoon vanilla extract

Blend all ingredients until smooth.

Blintzes, *like crepes, are cooked in their own special, long-handled skillet.*

Scandinavia

Christmas Menu

Sillsallad (Herring Salad), Sweden
Små Köttbullar (Small Swedish Meatballs), Sweden
Leverpastej (Swedish Liver Pâté), Sweden
Gaasesteg Med Aebler Og Svedsker
(Roast Goose with Apples and Prunes), Denmark
Brunede Kartofler (Caramelized Potatoes), Denmark
Rødkaal (Braised Red Cabbage), Denmark
Risgrynsgröt (Christmas Porridge), Sweden
Pepparkakor (Gingersnaps), Sweden
Julekage (Scandinavian Christmas Bread)
Glögg (Christmas Wine), Sweden
Coffee

RECOMMENDED WINES

Fumé Blanc
Cabernet Sauvignon
White Riesling

Additional Recipes

Smørrebrød (Open-Faced Sandwiches), Denmark
Ärter Med Fläsk (Yellow Pea Soup with Pork), Sweden
Fruktsoppa (Swedish Fruit Soup), Sweden
Jansson's Frestelse (Jansson's Temptation), Sweden
Plättar (Swedish Pancakes), Sweden
Saffransbröd (Swedish Saffron Bread), Sweden

A group of stalwart Swedes sets sail from New York harbor for Chicago.

e had a Swid parti last Sandi nait and de must fun." So Emma Anderson, a Swedish housemaid in turn-of-the-century America, wrote home in a dauntless attempt at phonetic English. In one sentence, she captured Scandinavian aptitude and attitude. The Scandinavians learned English eagerly, and brought a lively capacity for enjoyment to their new home. "We had fun then, with all there was to do," recalled one homesteader. "Lots of fun, lots of hard work," summed up another. A third, watching farmers work fields he had claimed seventy years before, observed, "It's easier now, but I don't think they are as happy as we were when I first cleared the land."

The first massive wave of immigrants from Scandinavia, principally Sweden and Norway, started in the late 1860s. Because of a nationwide harvest failure, rural Swedes were starving. Nearly half the country's mushrooming population was landless; small homesteads had been subdivided out of existence. In the midst of famine, nothing looked more promising than America's Homestead Act of 1862, which offered 160 acres free to any settler. Many immigrants felt they had little choice; a saying of the day was: "Swedish skin and bones in Sweden, or Swedish flesh and blood in America."

Norway, like Sweden, felt the pressure of too many people and not enough acreage, but her economy was stronger and more diversified. What her peasant class found intolerable was political and cultural domination by a small, arrogant middle class. Norwegians, perhaps more than other Scandinavians, set sail for America because it promised social equality. "Here it is not asked what or who was your father," one wrote, "but what are you?"

In the beginning, young families immigrated en masse to the homesteading towns of the Midwest, especially in Illinois, Minnesota and Wisconsin, and gradually spread to the Mississippi Valley, the Dakotas and Nebraska. The farther into the heartland they traveled, the less America looked like home. A photograph of the first plowing on Joseph Hansson's land in South Dakota, around 1910, shows something resembling a dark runway, long and narrow, stretching into an empty horizon. Anna Ohlson, a Norwegian who arrived in the Dakotas as a little girl in 1906, recalled that her mother "was always talking about the mountains and the fjords. She was homesick, I guess."

Some immigrants found the Midwest beautiful simply for its fertility. "Your finest plow lands at home cannot compare with the rich prairies here, where golden harvests grow," one farmer announced. Others, like Ida Lindgren, called it "desolate." Ida arrived in Kansas with her husband and five children in 1870. Her days were exhausting rounds of cooking, washing and baking; she grew "more or less used" to wheat bread but longed for "really good sour-sweet rye bread." Yellow peas, a Swedish staple grown and sold locally, brightened her dinners when the Lindgrens could afford them.

Ida survived extremes of weather unknown in her homeland, and in 1874 she watched grasshoppers ravage every green, growing thing for miles. "Only the peach stones still hung on the trees," she reported. Still, in the spirit of most Scandinavians, she found time for fun, playing Swedish games with her children and doing a "curtsy polka" up to the spring for a drink of water. "My heart," she wrote, "still rises up from time to time."

By the 1880s, Danes had brought their expertise as dairymen to Iowa and Wisconsin, and a second wave of Swedes and Norwegians was settling the Middle and Far West. Scandinavian contractors and crews built railroads and reputations for vigor as they helped link America to the Pacific in 1893. When James J. Hill, a railroad promoter and financier, started building the Great Northern, he proclaimed: "Give me Swedes, snuff and whiskey, and I'll build a railroad right through hell."

Once the railroad opened up the Northwest, children of the first Scandinavian wave were quick to follow, along with newly arrived immigrants. Oregon and especially the Puget Sound in Washington looked and felt like home. Scandinavians swiftly became leaders in the familiar trades of fishing and shipbuilding, and all along the West Coast immigrant lumbermen kept the legend of Paul Bunyan sharp as an ax. Another legendary figure, K. O. Erickson from Sweden, settled as a fur trader among Washington's Quillayute Indians, became an honorary chief and founded one of the first successful savings and loan associations in the country.

Farther north, the Klondike called as clearly as an old-country violin, and Scandinavians made a flamboyant entrance to the fortune seeker's ball. In 1896, Charles John Anderson, "The Lucky Swede," bought claim No. 29 on Eldorado Creek for 800 dollars from three disenchanted men and mined it for nearly 1.5 million dollars in gold. Two years later, three amateur Swedish prospectors made what was considered the first major gold strike in northern Alaska at Anvil Creek, the future site of Nome.

While Swedes kicked off the gold rush in the frozen north, a fresh group of Scandinavian immigrants poured through Ellis Island: young, single men and women in search of urban employment. Norwegians headed for Brooklyn, Danes and Swedes for Chicago, which by 1900 was the second largest Swedish city in the world. Probably no group left the homeland more willingly than

Scandinavian immigrants show off their catch of plump salmon from the Columbia River .

13624—First Haul of the Season—Salmon Industry, Columbia River, Oregon, U. S. A.

Swedish housemaids, unredeemed Cinderellas who often had to sleep in the kitchen. "Work every minute from 6 o'clock in the morning until 9 at night, Sundays and weekdays, always the same," one described it. When she reached America and kinder working conditions, she was "ashamed to get paid for what little I did."

Urban or rural, housemaid or lumberjack, Scandinavians shared the same approach to their new nation: In private they kept to themselves. Swedes resisted intermarriage. Norwegians, though they might fight the Irish for a bride, created an insular string of communities from Illinois to the Dakotas.

Yet publicly Scandinavians as a whole assimilated rapidly, especially the Danes, who came in smaller numbers and settled widely. They were literate and quick to speak English (though as one correspondent noted, "To try and read English is like putting Latin in front of the cat"). They were comfortable with Anglo-Saxon customs and deeply appreciative of democracy.

9334—Fishermen at Home, Columbia River, Oregon.

Miles of netting dry as these Scandinavian fishermen make necessary repairs on a wharf on the Columbia River.

Scandinavians were also, despite their initial reserve, a warm, hospitable people who brought graceful touches, games and laughter to their surroundings. To receive visitors meant, at the very least, to feed them cookies and coffee and more often to sit them down at a table glowing with candles and flowers for a hearty meat-and-potatoes meal. Christmas, a peerless excuse for festivities, could stretch into a long and merry month.

It was ushered in by St. Lucia Day on December 13, a holiday still observed in Scandinavian-American enclaves. According to an ancient calendar, December 13 marks the end of the longest night in the year. On that morning, a "Lucia bride," usually a daughter of the house, rises early, dresses in a white gown and a green wreath crowned with lit candles and serves her family coffee and Lucia buns in bed while singing a traditional song. Like the Scandinavians who left home to build a better life in America, she celebrates the gradual return of light.

SILLSALLAD

Herring Salad
6 SERVINGS

1   pound herring (salt, matjes, pickled or fillets in wine sauce), drained and chopped
2   cups chopped cooked beets
1½ cups chopped boiled potatoes
1   cup chopped apple
⅓   cup finely chopped dill pickle
¼   cup chopped onion
3   tablespoons white wine vinegar
2   tablespoons chopped fresh dill
1   tablespoon sugar
½   teaspoon salt
⅛   teaspoon freshly ground white pepper

TO SERVE:

½   cup heavy cream

Combine herring, beets, potatoes, apple, pickle and onion in large mixing bowl. Combine vinegar, 1 tablespoon of the dill, sugar, salt and pepper in small bowl and mix with fork until sugar dissolves. Pour over herring mixture and toss lightly to mix. Cover and refrigerate at least 1 hour to blend flavors.

Just before serving, whip cream to soft peaks and fold into salad. Sprinkle with remaining 1 tablespoon dill.

LEVERPASTEJ

Swedish Liver Pâté
16 APPETIZER SERVINGS

2   tablespoons butter
2   tablespoons flour
1   cup heavy cream
¾   cup milk
1   pound fresh calf's liver
1¼ pounds fresh pork fat
½   cup chopped onion
4   flat anchovy fillets, drained and coarsely chopped
3   eggs
1   teaspoon salt
½   teaspoon freshly ground white pepper
½   teaspoon ground allspice
½   teaspoon dried majoram, crumbled

¼   teaspoon ground ginger
¼   pound fresh mushrooms, chopped
¼   cup dry white wine

TO SERVE:

Thinly sliced rye bread
Crisp-cooked bacon strips
Sautéed fresh sliced mushrooms

Melt butter in small saucepan over medium heat. Stir in flour and cook and stir until bubbly. Whisk cream and milk into flour mixture. Contin-

Leverpastej is served Swedish-style—spread on thin slices of rye bread with bacon strips and mushrooms.

ue cooking and stirring until sauce comes to boil, then boil 1 minute. Remove from heat; cover and reserve.

Cut liver and ½ pound of the pork fat into 1-inch chunks and place in food processor bowl fitted with metal blade. Add onion, anchovies and ½ cup of the white sauce. Process to a smooth puree, stopping machine frequently to scrape down sides and gradually add remaining white sauce. Add all remaining ingredients, through wine, except remaining pork fat, then process until thoroughly blended.

Cut remaining pork fat lengthwise into ⅛-inch-wide strips. Arrange overlapping strips to cover bottom and sides of 9 × 5-inch loaf pan or 2-quart metal mold, reserving enough strips to cover top. Pour liver mixture into prepared pan and cover with reserved fat strips.

Cover pan with heavy-duty aluminum foil and place in large baking pan. Pour boiling water into baking pan to depth of 2 inches. Bake in preheated 350°F. oven until sharp knife inserted into center comes out clean, about 2 hours. Remove loaf pan from water and place on cooling rack. Uncover and cool to room temperature. Cover again with foil and refrigerate until thoroughly chilled, at least 4 hours. Remove pâté from pan. Cut into ½-inch slices. Serve on thin slices of rye bread. Garnish each serving with a bacon strip and mushroom slices.

SMÅ KÖTTBULLAR

Small Swedish Meatballs

3½ DOZEN APPETIZER MEATBALLS

¼   cup grated onion
3   tablespoons butter
1   pound lean ground beef
½   pound ground pork
½   cup cold mashed potatoes
¼   cup fine dry bread crumbs
3   tablespoons heavy cream
2   eggs, beaten
1½   teaspoons finely chopped fresh parsley
½   teaspoon salt
¼   teaspoon freshly ground black pepper
2   tablespoons vegetable oil
1½   tablespoons all-purpose flour
½   cup milk
     Salt and freshly ground pepper to taste

Sauté onion in 1 tablespoon of the butter over medium heat until soft, about 3 minutes. Combine onion, beef, pork, potatoes, bread crumbs, cream, eggs, parsley, salt and pepper in large mixing bowl. Mix with clean hands or wooden spoon until well blended. Shape into balls, using a slightly rounded measuring teaspoonful, and place on baking sheet. Cover with plastic wrap and refrigerate at least 1 hour.

Cook meatballs, half at a time, in remaining 2 tablespoons butter and the oil in large skillet over medium-high heat, turning frequently, until brown on all sides, 5 to 7 minutes. Remove meatballs to heated platter. Drain all but 1 tablespoon fat from skillet. Stir in flour and cook, stirring, 1 to 2 minutes. Gradually stir in milk. Heat to boiling over medium-high heat, stirring constantly. Boil 2 to 3 minutes. Add salt and pepper to taste and pour gravy over meatballs. Serve hot.

NOTE: To make larger, main-dish meatballs, use 1 level tablespoonful of meat mixture to shape balls. Cook as directed, increasing browning time to 10 to 12 minutes. Makes about 2 dozen.

GAASESTEG MED AEBLER OG SVEDSKER

Roast Goose with Apples and Prunes

8 SERVINGS

1	*ready-to-cook young goose (8 to 10 pounds), thawed if frozen*
	Half of one lemon
1	*teaspoon salt*
¼	*teaspoon freshly ground white pepper*
4	*medium cooking apples, cored and quartered*
20	*dried prunes, pitted*
1	*large onion, quartered*

Rinse goose under cool running water and pat dry with paper towels. Rub cavity with lemon and sprinkle with salt and pepper. Stuff cavity with apples, prunes and onion. Close opening with small metal skewers or sew with heavy thread. Fasten neck skin under back of goose with skewer. Place goose, breast side up, on rack in shallow roasting pan.

Insert meat thermometer in thigh of goose, away from bone. Roast in preheated 350°F. oven until thermometer registers 185°F. and juices run clear, 3 to 3½ hours, or about 25 minutes per pound. If necessary, cover loosely with aluminum foil during last hour of roasting to prevent excess browning. Remove skewers and discard stuffing. Let goose stand 10 minutes before carving.

Pour pan drippings into 2-cup measure. Remove and discard fat. Add water to remaining drippings if necessary to make 1½ cups liquid. Return liquid to roasting pan and heat to boiling over medium-high heat. Boil, stirring frequently, until mixture is reduced by half. Serve hot with goose.

OVERLEAF: *The traditional Danish recipe for roast goose calls for a stuffing of tart apples, dried prunes and onions.*

Min Bestefader
Hans Flakkeskaug's
tale til Kong Oskar
paa Lens Station
(Jernbanens aab...

1. Orrtupp. 2. Orrhöna. 3. Järpe. 4. Tjädertupp. 5. Tjäderhöna.

Served with its own rich pan juices, Gaasesteg med Abeler og Svedsker *goes well with Cabernet Sauvignon.*

BRUNEDE KARTOFLER

Caramelized Potatoes
6 TO 8 SERVINGS

1   *pound small new boiling potatoes*
½   *cup sugar*
8   *tablespoons butter, melted*
1   *tablespoon finely chopped fresh parsley*

Heat 6 cups water to boiling in 3-quart saucepan over medium-high heat. Add potatoes and cook until almost tender, 15 to 20 minutes. Remove from heat and let stand 15 minutes. Drain and pare potatoes.

Melt sugar in 10-inch skillet over medium-low heat, stirring constantly, about 5 minutes. Reduce heat to low and cook, stirring constantly, until sugar is light brown, about 1 minute longer. Stir in melted butter. Add half the potatoes. Cook, shaking pan constantly to coat potatoes evenly, for 3 to 4 minutes. Transfer glazed potatoes to serving dish. Repeat procedure with remaining potatoes. Spoon any caramel mixture remaining in skillet over potatoes. Sprinkle with parsley. Serve hot.

RØDKAAL

Braised Red Cabbage
6 SERVINGS

1   *medium head red cabbage (about 1½*
        pounds), thinly sliced
2   *tablespoons butter*
2   *medium cooking apples, cored and*
        chopped
¼   *cup apple juice or water*
3   *tablespoons dry red wine*
2   *tablespoons cider vinegar*
2   *tablespoons light molasses*
2   *tablespoons currant jelly*
½   *teaspoon salt*

Sauté cabbage in butter in 5-quart Dutch oven over medium heat, stirring frequently, until just softened, about 5 minutes. Stir in remaining ingredients. Reduce heat to medium-low, cover and cook until cabbage is tender, about 10 minutes. Serve hot.

RISGRYNSGRÖT

Christmas Porridge
6 SERVINGS

5   *cups milk*
1   *tablespoon butter*
1   *cup long-grain white rice*
5   *tablespoons sugar*
1   *teaspoon salt*
1   *teaspoon vanilla extract*
¼   *teaspoon ground cinnamon*

Bring milk and butter to a boil in 3-quart saucepan over medium-high heat. Stir in rice, 4 tablespoons of the sugar and the salt. Reduce heat to low. Cover and simmer until rice is soft but not mushy, 25 to 30 minutes. Pour rice into serving bowl and stir in vanilla. Mix together remaining 1 tablespoon sugar and cinnamon and sprinkle over porridge. Let stand about 30 minutes before serving.

PEPPARKAKOR

Gingersnaps
7 DOZEN

⅔   *cup light brown sugar*
⅔   *cup light molasses*
2   *teaspoons ground ginger*
1   *teaspoon ground cinnamon*
1   *teaspoon ground cardamom*
½   *teaspoon ground cloves*
12   *tablespoons butter, cut up*
2   *eggs*
5½   *cups all-purpose flour (approximately)*
½   *teaspoon baking soda*

Combine brown sugar, molasses and spices in 1½-quart saucepan. Heat to boiling over medium-high heat, stirring constantly. Boil 1 minute, then remove from heat.

Place butter in large mixing bowl, add hot sugar mixture and stir until butter melts. Blend in eggs.

Stir 2 cups flour and the baking soda together. Gradually mix into the butter mixture. Mix in enough additional flour to make stiff dough. Shape dough into ball. Wrap in plastic wrap and refrigerate several hours or overnight.

Cut dough into quarters. Shape one quarter at a time into balls (refrigerate other dough). Use rounded teaspoonful of dough for each ball. Place on ungreased cookie sheets. Bake in preheated 350°F. oven until light brown, 10 to 12 minutes. Cool on wire racks. Store in airtight container.

NOTE: To make cut-out cookies, place each quarter of dough on large ungreased cookie sheet and roll out to ⅛-inch thick-

Cut into a variety of festive shapes, Gingersnaps *are a special part of Scandinavian Christmas festivities.*

ness. Cut into desired shapes with cookie cutters. Remove scraps of dough from between cookies. Reroll scraps on lightly floured surface, cut out and transfer to cookie sheet with wide metal spatula. Bake only 6 to 8 minutes. Makes about 5 dozen cookies.

JULEKAGE

Scandinavian Christmas Bread

2 LOAVES

4½ cups all-purpose flour, plus additional
     1 cup as needed
2 packages (¼ ounce each) active dry
     yeast (2 scant tablespoons)
1½ teaspoons ground cardamom
½ cup milk
½ cup granulated sugar
4 tablespoons butter, cut up
1 teaspoon salt
1 teaspoon grated lemon rind
2 eggs
1½ cups diced candied fruit
½ cup golden raisins
¼ cup chopped walnuts (optional)
     Oil

FOR GLAZE:

1 cup sifted powdered sugar
1½ tablespoons milk

Stir together 2 cups of the flour, yeast and cardamom in large mixing bowl. Heat milk, ½ cup water, sugar, butter, salt and lemon rind in small saucepan over low heat just until warm (115° to 120°F.). Add to dry mixture. Beat until smooth, about 2 minutes on medium speed of electric mixer or 300 strokes by hand. Beat in eggs, candied fruit, raisins and walnuts, if desired. Add 1 cup flour and beat 1 minute on medium speed or 150 strokes by hand. Stir in enough additional flour to make a moderately stiff dough.

Turn dough onto lightly floured surface and knead until smooth and satiny, 10 to 12 minutes. Shape dough into ball and place in lightly greased bowl, turning to grease all sides. Cover and let rise in warm place (80° to 85°F.) until doubled in bulk, about 1½ hours.

Punch dough down, cover and let rest 10 minutes. Divide in half. Shape each half into smooth ball and place on greased baking sheet. Roll or pat into circle 8 inches in diameter and brush with oil. Cover and let stand in warm place until doubled in bulk, about 1 hour.

Bake in preheated 350°F. oven until evenly browned, 25 to 30 minutes. Remove loaves to wire racks and cool.

Blend powdered sugar and milk until smooth. Spread over cooled loaves.

SMØRREBRØD

Open-Faced Sandwiches

Smørrebrød, meaning "buttered bread," is the splendid open-faced sandwich that—in its infinite varieties—represents the typical Danish luncheon.

This Danish invention is really much more than a sandwich. Each consists of a single thin slice of firm, buttered bread topped with two or more ingredients. The choice of toppings, called *paaleg*, literally "something laid on," is almost limitless. All that matters is that the ingredients complement one another in flavor and texture, and that they are arranged attractively on the bread.

Although the true story behind the invention of smørrebrød remains a mystery, legend has it that it evolved as early as the eighteenth century, when rounds of bread took the place of plates. The bread rounds, soaked with meat juices, were eaten as part of the main course or, with the addition of honey, as dessert.

The Danish expertise in the preparation of smørrebrød seems to have been passed on from generation to generation. The final product, eaten with knife and fork, is really a work of art. The first layer of ingredients, placed over the buttered bread, might be slices of meat, seafood salad, fried fish fillets, sliced hard-cooked egg, cheese, slices of cold boiled potato or leftovers from the previous night's meal. Over this, any of several garnishes will be arranged: onion rings, dill or parsley sprigs, asparagus tips, sliced pickled beets, chopped tomato, chopped or sliced gherkins, aspic cubes, or anchovy fillets.

Here are a few examples of the dozens of smørrebrød that can be quickly assembled from readily available ingredients:

Danish liver pâté with sautéed mushroom slices and crisp bacon on rye bread.

Tiny shrimp on lettuce, topped with sliced cucumber, on white bread.

Sliced hard-cooked eggs and tomatoes with chopped chives on rye bread.

Smoked salmon on lettuce, with scrambled egg and horseradish sauce, on rye bread.

Sliced roast beef with fried egg and onion rings on pumpernickel bread.

Sliced pork loin with cold sliced beets on white bread.

GLÖGG

Christmas Wine
2½ QUARTS (20 SERVINGS)

2   bottles (750ml each) dry red wine
1   bottle (750ml) Swedish aquavit or
      vodka
½   cup granulated sugar
1½ cups golden raisins
4   whole cardamom pods
10 whole cloves
2   sticks cinnamon, broken into halves
      Peel from 1 orange
1½ cups blanched whole almonds
1   cup sugar cubes

FOR GARNISH:

Orange slices

Combine 1 bottle wine, 1 cup aquavit, granulated sugar and raisins in 4-quart saucepan. Remove seeds from cardamom pods and tie the seeds in three layers of cheesecloth with cloves, cinnamon and orange peel. Add to wine mixture. Heat to boiling over high heat. Reduce heat to low, cover and simmer 15 minutes. Remove and discard cheesecloth bag. Stir in remaining wine and almonds.

Heat ½ cup aquavit in small saucepan over low heat just until warm.

Place sugar cubes in larger saucepan. Pour aquavit over sugar cubes and immediately ignite with long wooden match. Gradually pour remaining aquavit over sugar cubes to keep flame burning. When sugar has melted, stir into wine mixture. Serve hot with an orange slice in each cup.

ÄRTER MED FLÄSK

Yellow Pea Soup with Pork
6 TO 8 SERVINGS

1   pound (2 cups) dried yellow Swedish
      peas or split peas, washed and sorted
2   pounds boneless pork shoulder
3   leeks, cleaned and chopped
2   medium onions, chopped
2   carrots, pared and shredded
2   teaspoons fresh parsley, chopped
1   teaspoon salt

1   teaspoon dried marjoram, crumbled
½   teaspoon dried thyme, crumbled
¼   teaspoon ground ginger

TO SERVE:

Spicy brown or Dijon mustard

Place peas and 7 cups cold water in 5-quart Dutch oven and heat to boiling

Glögg is a traditional Scandinavian holiday drink.

over high heat. Boil 2 minutes, remove from heat and let peas soak 30 minutes. Add all remaining ingredients except mustard to pot. Cover and heat to boiling over high heat. Reduce heat to low. Simmer, partially covered, until pork and peas are tender, about 1 to 1½ hours.

Remove pork from soup, cut into thin slices and arrange on serving plate. Serve with mustard. Ladle soup into individual bowls. Serve hot.

FRUKTSOPPA

Swedish Fruit Soup
8 SERVINGS

¾   cup pitted dried apricots
¾   cup pitted dried prunes
½   cup sugar
3   tablespoons quick-cooking tapioca
2   tablespoons currant jelly
3   thick lemon slices
2   whole cloves
1   stick cinnamon
¼   cup golden raisins
1   tart apple, cored, pared and cubed

Soak apricots and prunes in 6 cups cold water in 3-quart saucepan for 30 minutes. Add sugar, tapioca, jelly, lemon, cloves and cinnamon and heat to boiling over high heat. Reduce heat to low. Cover and cook until fruits are tender, about 10 minutes. Stir in raisins and apple and cook 5 minutes longer. Remove from heat; and cool to room temperature.

Place soup in large glass bowl. Discard cloves and cinnamon. Cover soup with plastic wrap and refrigerate until chilled, at least 2 hours. Serve cold.

JANSSON'S FRESTELSE

Jansson's Temptation
6 SERVINGS

6   medium boiling potatoes
3   cups thinly sliced onions
4   tablespoons butter
1   tablespoon vegetable oil
1   2-ounce can flat anchovy fillets
⅛   teaspoon freshly ground white pepper
1   cup heavy cream
3   tablespoons milk
2   tablespoons fine dry bread crumbs

Pare potatoes and cut into strips approximately 2 inches long and ¼ inch wide. Immerse in cold water to prevent discoloration.

Sauté onions in 2 tablespoons of the butter and the oil until soft. Drain and chop anchovies.

Drain potatoes and pat dry with paper towels. Arrange one-third of potatoes in greased 2-quart baking dish.

Top with half the onions and sprinkle with half the anchovies and half the pepper. Repeat layers, ending with potatoes. Combine cream and milk and pour over potatoes.

Sprinkle with bread crumbs. Cut remaining butter into small pieces and sprinkle over crumbs.

Bake in preheated 400°F. oven until potatoes are fork-tender in center and most of liquid is absorbed, 45 to 55 minutes. Serve hot.

PLÄTTAR

Swedish Pancakes
8 SERVINGS

3   eggs
2   cups heavy cream
1   cup all-purpose flour
1   tablespoon sugar
½   teaspoon salt
4   tablespoons unsalted butter, melted

Melted butter (for pan)

TO SERVE:

1   14½-ounce jar sweetened wild
    lingonberries

Fresh lingonberries add distinctive color and flavor to Swedish Pancakes.

Beat eggs with whisk in large mixing bowl. Beat in cream, flour, sugar and salt. Whisk until smooth, then blend in 4 tablespoons melted butter.

Heat large skillet or Swedish pancake pan over medium-high heat. Brush lightly with melted butter and drop batter onto pan by tablespoonful. Cook until golden brown on bottom, about 2 minutes. Turn and cook 1 to 2 minutes longer. Keep cooked pancakes warm in preheated 225°F. oven while preparing remaining pancakes. Serve with lingonberries.

SAFFRANSBRÖD

Swedish Saffron Bread
40 BUNS

3½ cups all-purpose flour, plus additional
  ½ cup as needed
1 package (¼ ounce) active dry yeast
  (1 scant tablespoon)
1 cup heavy cream
⅓ cup sugar
4 tablespoons butter
½ teaspoon salt
⅛ teaspoon powdered saffron
2 eggs
  Dark raisins
  Oil

Stir together 1½ cups of the flour and the yeast in large mixing bowl. Heat cream, sugar, butter, salt and saffron in small saucepan over low heat just until warm (115° to 120°F.). Add to flour mixture. Beat until smooth, about 2 minutes on medium speed of electric mixer or 300 strokes by hand. Beat in 1 egg. Stir in enough additional flour to make moderately stiff dough.

Turn dough onto lightly floured surface and knead until smooth and satiny, 8 to 10 minutes. Shape dough into ball and place in lightly greased bowl, turning to grease all sides. Cover and let rise in warm place (80° to 85°F.) until doubled in bulk, about 1½ hours.

Punch dough down, cover and let rest 10 minutes. Divide into quarters and cut each into 10 equal pieces. Roll each piece between palms and work surface to make 12-inch rope. On greased cookie sheet, shape each rope into an "S"-shaped bun, coiling ends snail-fashion. Place a raisin in center of each coil. Brush lightly with oil. Cover and let stand in warm place until doubled in bulk, 30 to 35 minutes.

Beat remaining egg and 2 tablespoons water with fork until blended and brush over rolls. Bake in preheated 375°F. oven until golden, 12 to 15 minutes. Remove buns to wire racks and cool completely.

The "S" shape characterizes golden brown Saffransbröd.

France

French Luncheon Menu

Pâté En Croûte (Pâté in Pastry)
Pain Français (French Bread)
Potage au Cresson (Watercress Soup)
Entrecôte Grillée à la Bordelaise (Broiled Steak with Red Wine Sauce)
Glace aux Fraises (Strawberry Ice Cream)
Café au Lait

RECOMMENDED WINES

Chardonnay
Cabernet Sauvignon

Additional Recipes

Coq au Riesling (Chicken in White Wine)
Boeuf Bourguignon (Beef Stew in Red Wine)
Ratatouille (Eggplant Casserole)
Pommes de Terre Dauphinois (Scalloped Potatoes)
Bouillabaisse (Fish Stew)
Soupe à l'Oignon Gratinée (Onion Soup)
Coquilles St. Jacques (Scallops in White Wine)
Brioche (Egg Bread)
Poires au Vin Rouge (Pears in Red Wine)

Jean Nicolet, the first European to see Lake Michigan, knew when he reached it that he would not find the Chinese city he was seeking. With the keen French instinct for drama, however, he dressed for the occasion anyway. He wore a gorgeous Oriental silk robe embroidered with birds and flowers and gripped a pistol in each hand as he stepped from his canoe. The Winnebagos, the people he had hoped would be Chinese, were dazzled. A crowd of 4,000 or 5,000 admirers gathered, and Nicolet's party was feted with 120 roasted beavers.

Gallic gestures, ranging from the elegant to the spectacular, continued to give the French in America an influence far out of proportion to their numbers. French immigration was the most stable of that of any European country, but it was also among the smallest; at times, the rate of repatriation exceeded the rate of arrival. Even so, the French contribution to America was as sweeping as independence and as subtle as fine wine.

French attempts at civilizing the American wilderness began with religious instruction. Samuel de Champlain, who discovered Quebec in 1608, believed exploration was only the first step toward bringing the true faith to every corner of the world. As a result, Catholic priests arrived in Quebec by 1615. They set off into the woods along the St. Lawrence River and the Great Lakes, their endurance surpassed only by their zeal. When the redoubtable Father Isaac Jogues, strapped to a scaffold by unfriendly Iroquois in 1641, was tossed an ear of green corn for sustenance, he used the raindrops on the husks to baptize two fellow prisoners. (He was eventually canonized.)

Explorers, fur traders, *coureurs de bois* ("runners of the woods") and devoted Jesuits paddled, portaged and bushwhacked their

French immigrants wait in line for an eye examination at Ellis Island.

way to places never before seen by Europeans, from the Great Lakes to the mouth of the Mississippi, where in 1682 Robert Cavelier de La Salle claimed "this country of Louisiana" for Louis XIV.

Shortly afterward, a less footloose group began emigrating from France: the Huguenots, whose Protestant beliefs had been outlawed when the Edict of Nantes was revoked in 1685. The Huguenots had tried America in the 1560s, but Spaniards had demolished their Florida settlement in the name of Catholic supremacy. They found conditions much improved in the eighteenth century, and 14,000 or so settled throughout the colonies, easing the transition by converting from unyielding Calvinism to American Anglicanism.

Regarded at home as a plain people, the Huguenots blossomed into leaders of style in America. Because many were highly skilled artisans, their homes were graced with exquisite silver, furniture, mirrors and carpets. They introduced yeast, buns, artichokes and tomatoes to American tables, and their vineyards flourished. Other colonists respected their drive and intelligence. In many ways, the Huguenots represented the general character of French immigration through the early twentieth century. Middle-class, educated and enterprising, they approached life in their new country as successful individuals, not as a community bound together by common hardships.

The same could not be said of the group France shipped from her prisons, asylums and streets in an attempt to increase the population of Louisiana. Not surprisingly, these unwilling immigrants failed to quicken the colony's growth. Forced emigration ceased after 1720, but voluntary colonization never gathered momentum, and the gigantic "country of Louisiana" held only

11,000 people when France ceded it to Spain in 1763.

During the last half of 1775, when the American revolt had been proclaimed an "open and avowed rebellion" by the British, the French government kept up a façade of indifference. But by 1776, secret shipments of French arms and ammunition were crossing the Atlantic, and two years later France openly allied herself with the colonies. The war ended in 1781 at the Battle of Yorktown. The French were so instrumental in the Continental victory that a British general tried to give the sword of surrender to the Comte de Rochambeau instead of George Washington. The Marquis de Lafayette, to clear up any misunderstanding, requested that the American band play "Yankee Doodle."

In the years after the war, American women showed a distinct preference for French fashions, and the first four American Presidents demonstrated a robust appreciation of French cuisine. John Adams found it "elegant," "mighty" and "sinful" (the latter notion ceased to bother him after a trip to France in 1778). Thomas Jefferson installed a French chef in the White House, won ecstatic compliments from guests and in what must have been a memorable year ran up a wine bill of $2,800.

The French Revolution brought a glittering group to the American wilds at the end of the eighteenth century: French monarchists who dreamed of establishing palatial estates in planned communities. The most successful colony was Asylum, Pennsylvania, where the *haut monde* built two-story log homes complete with glass windows, chimneys and landscaping. These fripperies, T. Wood Clark wrote in *Emigrés in the Wilderness*, convinced homespun natives that "the Frenchmen were insane." Asylum's inhabitants worked behind shop counters and plows by day and donned full evening dress for music, cards and dancing at night, awaiting the day, which came in 1802, when they would be beckoned back to France. Intriguing evidence suggests that Louis XVII, the "Lost Dauphin," was spirited out of prison and brought to America in 1795, to be raised under the name of Eleazar Williams.

A different class of Frenchmen continued to push the frontier west: the river men, trappers and fur traders who became America's legendary mountain men in the early nineteenth century. Cheerful, tough and diplomatic, they got along famously with the Indians, married Indian women and came to reckon time "from the flood of the river or the ripening of the strawberries." French mountain men guided scientific, military and survey expeditions until the 1880s.

On the West Coast, a Frenchman from Bordeaux named Jean-Louis Vignes reckoned time by the ripening of some of the first grapes planted in California. By 1833 his wines and brandies were winning acclaim, in plenty of time to assuage the needs of the 30,000 French lured by the Gold Rush.

Most of the newcomers from France in the nineteenth and early twentieth centuries, however, had more prosaic plans. Teaching and cooking consistently led the list of French-American professions; doctors, engineers, architects and natural scientists came seeking advanced technologies. And there was always a market for French luxury items: wine, chocolates, jewelry, clothing, cosmetics and perfume.

The most indelible expression of French-American relations was conceived in 1865, at the home of Édouard René de Laboulaye, near Versailles. Laboulaye's guests, who included the sculptor Auguste Bartholdi, decided the French should give the Americans a gift, not from one government to another, but from one people to another in recognition of shared values.

French fund raising for the gift began in 1875. Everyone from ordinary citizens to the president of the Third Republic contributed. Inspired by a visit to New York, Bartholdi set to work on "a bold and clear design" for a sculpture, using his mother, Charlotte, as a model. Alexandre Gustave Eiffel engineered the sculpture's strong, flexible iron skeleton. Meanwhile, across the Atlantic, thousands of Americans began donating money for the pedestal.

On October 28, 1886, almost precisely 105 years after the victory at Yorktown, hundreds of thousands of people turned their eyes toward a mist-shrouded island in New York Harbor where Bartholdi waited. He pulled a French flag from the massive face of his sculpture—and the Statue of Liberty began her steadfast gaze over the Atlantic, holding the light of freedom high in the grandest Gallic gesture of all.

French-American children celebrate their first Fourth of July.

PÂTÉ EN CROÛTE

Pâté in Pastry

18 TO 20 SERVINGS

3/4   pound lean ground veal
3/4   pound lean ground pork
6   ounces calves liver, ground
3   ounces fresh pork fat, ground
1   ounce imported truffles (drained if
      canned), finely chopped, (optional)
4   tablespoons cognac
1/4   cup finely chopped onion
1/4   cup finely chopped shallots
1   small clove garlic, finely chopped
2   tablespoons unsalted butter
1   egg, beaten
1/4   cup crème fraîche or heavy cream
1   tablespoon all-purpose flour
1   teaspoon salt
1   teaspoon fresh lemon juice
1/2   teaspoon dried thyme, crumbled
1/4   teaspoon ground allspice
1/4   teaspoon freshly ground black pepper
      Butter Pastry (recipe follows)

Combine veal, pork, liver, pork fat and truffles in large bowl. Mix thoroughly. Sprinkle with 2 tablespoons cognac.

Sauté onion, shallots and garlic in butter in small skillet over medium heat until soft but not browned, about 5 minutes. Add to meat mixture. Add remaining cognac to pan drippings and cook until reduced to 1 tablespoon. Add to meat mixture. Reserve 2 teaspoons beaten egg in small bowl. Add remaining egg and all remaining ingredients except *But-*

ter Pastry. Mix thoroughly.

Cut off about 1/3 of dough for butter pastry, cover and reserve. Roll remaining dough on lightly floured surface into circle 13 to 14 inches in diameter. Fit circle into lightly greased 8- or 9-inch springform pan. Spread meat mixture evenly over pastry.

Roll out remaining pastry into circle to 9 to 10 inches in diameter. Place over meat mixture in pan. Trim excess pastry, reserving trimmings. Pinch edges of pastry together around sides to seal in meat mixture. Reroll trimmings to 1/8-inch thickness. Cut out pastry into decorative shapes. Brush top of pastry lightly with remaining beaten egg. Arrange cutouts over pastry in attractive design. Brush with beaten egg. Insert meat thermometer into center of pâté.

Place on shelf in lower third of preheated 400°F. oven. Reduce temperature to 350°F. Bake until pâté is cooked (internal temperature of 180°F.), about 2 hours. Cool on rack at room temperature 3 to 4 hours. (Pastry will soften if pâté is refrigerated too soon.) Refrigerate until thoroughly chilled, at least 6 to 8 hours. To serve, cut into 1/2-inch-thick slices.

The golden crust is artfully decorated, but the treasure rests inside—rich pâté flavored with truffles and ognac.

BUTTER PASTRY

3 *cups all-purpose flour*
1 *teaspoon salt*
5½ *tablespoons chilled, unsalted butter,
     cut up*
½ *cup vegetable shortening*
1 *egg, beaten*

Stir flour and salt together into medium bowl. Cut in butter and shortening with pastry blender or 2 knives until mixture resembles coarse crumbs. Blend together egg and 4 tablespoons ice water. Sprinkle over dry mixture. Mix lightly with fork just until dough begins to stick together. (Add more water as needed.) Press dough into ball.

PAIN FRANÇAIS

French Bread
1 LOAF

1 *package active dry yeast (1 scant
     tablespoon)*
1 *teaspoon sugar*
3 *cups all-purpose flour*
1 *teaspoon salt*

Combine ¼ cup warm water (105° to 115°F.), yeast and sugar in small bowl. Stir to dissolve yeast. Let stand until bubbly, about 5 minutes. Measure flour and salt into large mixing bowl. Add yeast mixture and ½ cup warm water. Mix, adding additional water as necessary, until moderately stiff dough forms. Turn dough onto lightly floured surface. Knead until smooth and satiny, 5 to 8 minutes. Shape into ball. Place in lightly greased bowl, turning to grease all sides. Cover and let rise in warm place (80° to 85°F.) until doubled in bulk, about 1½ hours.

Punch dough down. Cover and let rise in warm place until doubled in bulk, about 1½ hours. Punch down again, cover and let rest 10 minutes. Pat dough out on lightly floured surface into rectangle about 12 inches long. Roll up, jelly-roll fashion, into 15-inch rope. Pinch ends and seam to seal. Place loaf diagonally, seam-side down, on large greased baking sheet. Cut 4 diagonal slashes, each 3 inches long, in dough, using very sharp knife or razor blade. Cover dough loosely with plastic wrap and let stand in warm place until almost doubled in bulk, about 45 minutes.

Place shallow pan of boiling water on bottom shelf of preheated 400°F. oven. Brush loaf lightly with water. Place on middle shelf of oven. Bake until loaf is golden and sounds hollow when tapped, about 30 minutes. Remove from baking sheet and cool on wire rack.

NOTE: To prepare dough in food processor, combine water, yeast and sugar and let stand as directed above. Measure flour and salt into work bowl fitted with steel blade. Process 10 seconds. Add yeast mixture and process 10 seconds. With motor running, slowly drizzle just enough remaining water through feed tube so that dough forms ball that cleans sides of bowl. Process 15 to 20 seconds. Turn off motor and let dough stand 2 minutes. Turn on motor and gradually drizzle in enough water to make dough that is smooth and satiny but not sticky. Process 10 to 15 seconds. Follow directions above for raising, shaping and baking bread.

POTAGE AU CRESSON

Watercress Soup
6 TO 8 SERVINGS

6   *cups rich homemade chicken broth*
1   *pound medium boiling potatoes, pared and thinly sliced*
1   *pound leeks, including tender green tops, cleaned and thinly sliced*
1   *small stalk celery, thinly sliced*
1   *medium onion, peeled and thinly sliced*
1   *cup watercress leaves and stems, packed (about ¼ pound), rinsed and drained*
   Salt
   Pepper

TO SERVE:

¾   *cup crème fraîche or heavy cream*

Place broth, potatoes, leeks, celery and onion in 4- or 5-quart saucepan. Bring to boil over high heat. Reduce heat to medium-low. Simmer, partially covered, until vegetables are tender, 40 to 45 minutes.

Reserve 6 small sprigs watercress. Stir remainder into soup and simmer 5 minutes. Strain soup, returning liquid to pan. Press vegetables through large sieve or food mill, or process until smooth in blender or food processor fitted with steel blade. Add to liquid in pan. Add salt and pepper to taste. To serve, stir in crème fraîche and garnish with reserved watercress.

POMMES DE TERRE DAUPHINOIS

Scalloped Potatoes
6 SERVINGS

1   *small clove garlic*
4   *tablespoons unsalted butter, chilled*
2   *pounds medium boiling potatoes*

½   *teaspoon salt*
⅛   *teaspoon freshly ground white pepper*
1   *cup (4 ounces) shredded Gruyère cheese*

½ cup heavy cream
½ cup milk

Bruise garlic with flat side of knife and rub over bottom and sides of oven-proof 1½ or 2-quart shallow baking dish. Coat dish evenly with about 1 teaspoon butter. Cut remaining butter into ¼-inch cubes and refrigerate while preparing potatoes.

Pare potatoes and slice ⅛ inch thick. Immediately immerse slices in cold water to prevent discoloration. When all potatoes are sliced, drain and pat dry with paper towels. Arrange half potatoes in dish and sprinkle with half the salt, half the pepper, half the cheese and half the butter. Top with remaining potatoes, salt, pepper, cheese and butter.

Combine cream and milk in small saucepan and bring to simmer over medium-high heat. Pour over potato mixture. Bake in preheated 425°F. oven until potatoes are tender, most liquid is absorbed and top is browned, 25 to 30 minutes. Serve hot.

ENTRECÔTE GRILLÉE À LA BORDELAISE

Broiled Steak with Red Wine Sauce
6 SERVINGS

2 tablespoons unsalted butter
2 tablespoons vegetable oil
1½ pounds boneless rib, club or sirloin
    steak, 1¼-inches thick
    Salt
    Freshly ground black pepper

TO SERVE:

    Bordelaise Sauce (recipe follows)
2 tablespoons finely chopped fresh parsley

Heat butter and oil in large heavy skillet until foam from butter begins to subside. Add steak and sauté 3 to 4 minutes. Turn and sauté to desired degree of doneness (3 to 4 minutes longer for medium-rare). Transfer to heated platter. Sprinkle with salt and pepper. Cover and keep warm.

In same skillet, prepare *Bordelaise Sauce.* Pour over meat. Sprinkle with parsley. Serve hot.

BORDELAISE SAUCE

3 pounds beef marrow bones, parboiled 30
    seconds
1 tablespoon unsalted butter
3 tablespoons finely chopped shallots
½ cup dry red wine
½ cup rich homemade beef broth
1 tablespoon cognac
1 small bay leaf
    Pinch dried thyme, crumbled
    Salt
    Freshly ground black pepper

The classic red wine sauce known as Bordelaise *is poured over a thick, juicy steak.*

Remove marrow from bones with small sharp knife dipped in hot water. Dice marrow.

Melt butter in pan drippings. Add shallots and cook 2 minutes over medium heat. Add wine, broth, cognac, bay leaf and thyme. Increase heat to medium-high. Cook, stirring to scrape up pan drippings, until liquid is reduced to about ½ cup, 4 to 5 minutes. Remove from heat and stir in marrow. Remove and discard bay leaf. Season with salt and pepper to taste.

COQ AU RIESLING

Chicken in White Wine

6 TO 8 SERVINGS

½   *pound small white onions*
1   *slice bacon, diced*
4   *tablespoons butter*
½   *pound mushrooms*
1   *roasting chicken (5 to 6 pounds), cut into serving pieces*
2   *tablespoons brandy*
3   *cups Riesling*
1   *cup rich homemade chicken broth*
2   *cloves garlic, peeled*
1   *sprig fresh thyme*
1   *bay leaf*
1   *sprig fresh parsley*
1   *celery leaf*
    Salt
    Freshly ground black pepper

Bring 2 cups water to boil over high heat in 1½-quart saucepan. Add onions and cook 2 minutes. Drain onions in colander and cool with cold running water. Peel and pat dry with paper towels. Cook bacon in butter in 5- or 6-quart stockpot or Dutch oven over medium-high heat just until bacon begins to brown, 3 to 5 minutes. Add onions and sauté, stirring frequently, until light brown, 8 to 10 minutes. Remove with slotted spoon.

Sauté mushrooms in butter in stockpot until just beginning to brown, about 5 minutes. Remove with slotted spoon and add to onions. Cover and refrigerate.

Sauté chicken pieces in butter until browned on all sides, about 15 minutes. Drizzle with brandy and quickly ignite with long wooden match. Burn until flames extinguish. Add wine, chicken broth, garlic, and herbs tied in cheesecloth bag. Cover and simmer over low heat until chicken is almost tender, about 1½ hours.

Add onions and mushrooms and simmer, uncovered, 30 minutes longer.

Remove chicken pieces, onions and mushrooms with slotted spoon. Arrange on heated serving platter and keep warm. Remove herbs and garlic. Skim off fat. Boil liquid over high heat until reduced to 1 cup. Season with salt and pepper to taste. Pour over chicken. Serve hot.

The French custom of serving the same wine used in cooking is exemplified by this Alsatian chicken dish, Coq au Riesling.

BOEUF BOURGUIGNON

Beef Stew in Red Wine
6 SERVINGS

3   ounces slab bacon, cut into 1½- x ¼-
      inch strips
2   tablespoons olive oil
3   pounds boneless lean beef rump, cut
      into 2-inch cubes
1   large carrot, pared and finely chopped
1   small onion, peeled and finely chopped
3   shallots, finely chopped
2   tablespoons all-purpose flour
2½ cups hot rich homemade beef broth
2   cups dry red wine
2   cloves garlic, finely chopped
1   tablespoon tomato paste
1   teaspoon dried thyme, crumbled
½   teaspoon salt
¼   teaspoon freshly ground black pepper
3   sprigs fresh parsley
1   bay leaf
18 to 24 small white onions, about 1 inch
      in diameter
4   tablespoons butter
1   tablespoon vegetable oil
½   pound fresh mushrooms, cleaned

TO SERVE:

2   tablespoons finely chopped fresh parsley

Bring 1 cup water to boil in 1½-quart saucepan over high heat. Add bacon. Reduce heat to medium-low and simmer 5 minutes. Drain bacon, discarding water, and pat dry with paper towels. Sauté bacon in olive oil in 5- or 6-quart casserole or Dutch oven over medium-high heat until lightly browned, 5 to 7 minutes. Remove with slotted spoon.

Pat beef cubes dry with paper towels. Cook, half at a time, in fat remaining in casserole. Stir frequently, until evenly browned, 8 to 10 minutes.

Remove beef from casserole. Reduce heat to medium and sauté carrot, onion and shallots in casserole until lightly browned, about 5 minutes. Stir in flour and cook stirring, 1 minute. Gradually whisk in beef broth, then stir in wine, garlic, tomato paste, thyme, salt and pepper. Tie parsley and bay leaf in cheesecloth bag and add to casserole with beef and bacon. Increase heat to high. Cover and bring to simmer. Place casserole in preheated 350°F. oven. Cook 1 hour, stirring occasionally. Uncover and cook until beef is tender, 1 to 1½ hours longer.

Bring 2 cups water to boil over high heat in 1½-quart saucepan. Add onions and cook 2 minutes. Drain onions in colander and cool with cold running water. Peel onions and pat dry with paper towels. Sauté in 2 tablespoons butter and vegetable oil in large skillet over medium heat, shaking pan frequently to roll onions around, until lightly browned on all sides, 8 to 10 minutes. Transfer to 1½-quart ovenproof casserole. Bake, uncovered, in 350°F. oven until tender, about 30 minutes.

Cut larger mushrooms into halves or quarters, leave small mushrooms whole. Sauté in 2 tablespoons butter in large skillet over medium heat, stirring frequently, until lightly browned, about 5 minutes. Add to baked onions. Cover.

When meat is tender, stir in onions and mushrooms. Bake 15 minutes longer. Discard herb bag. Skim off fat. Serve directly from casserole, or transfer to heated serving platter. To serve, sprinkle with parsley.

RATATOUILLE

Eggplant Casserole
6 TO 8 SERVINGS

2   small eggplants (about 1 pound each), pared and sliced ½ inch thick
     Salt
2   medium zucchini (about 1 pound), sliced ¼ inch thick
½   cup olive oil
2   green peppers, seeded and diced
2   medium onions, peeled and sliced ¼ inch thick
2   cloves garlic, finely chopped
2   pounds ripe tomatoes, peeled, seeded and chopped
¼   cup chopped fresh parsley
     Freshly ground black pepper

Place eggplant slices in colander and sprinkle lightly with salt. Let stand 30 minutes.

Sauté zucchini in 2 tablespoons oil in large heavy skillet over medium-high heat until golden on both sides, about 5 minutes. Remove from skillet.

Add 1 tablespoon oil to skillet, then add peppers and sauté until lightly browned, about 2 minutes. Remove from skillet. Add 1 more tablespoon oil if necessary, then add onions and sauté until transparent, 6 to 8 minutes, stirring to separate slices into rings. Remove from skillet.

Rinse eggplant slices under cold running water. Drain well and pat dry with paper towels. Add garlic and all but 1 teaspoon remaining oil to skillet. Sauté until garlic is tender, 3 to 5 minutes. Add tomatoes and boil until most liquid has evaporated, 4 to 6 minutes.

Arrange eggplant slices over tomatoes, then layer with peppers, onions and zucchini. Sprinkle with parsley, salt and pepper to taste. Cover and simmer over medium-low heat until almost all liquid has evaporated, about 15 minutes. Serve hot, at room temperature or chilled.

OVERLEAF: Bouillabaisse *combines a variety of Mediterranean fish and seafood in a saffron-scented tomato broth.*

BOUILLABAISSE

Fish Stew
8 SERVINGS

16   slices French bread, each ¾-inch thick
4   pounds assorted fish and shellfish
        (see Note)
     Fish Stock (recipe follows)
2   large onions, sliced ¼ inch thick
4   cloves garlic, finely chopped
½   cup olive oil
1   pound ripe tomatoes, peeled, seeded and
        chopped
⅛   teaspoon powdered saffron
1   strip dried orange rind
1   bay leaf
1   spring fresh thyme
1   sprig fresh parsley
1   sprig fresh fennel leaf

TO SERVE:

½   cup chopped fresh parsley
     Rouille (recipe follows)

Arrange bread in single layer on baking sheet. Bake in preheated 325°F. oven until dry and lightly toasted, about 20 to 30 minutes.

Cut fish into chunks, reserving bones, tails, heads and other trimmings for stock. Cover and reserve.

Prepare *Fish Stock*.

Sauté onions and garlic in oil in large skillet over medium heat until tender, 8 to 10 minutes. Add tomatoes, saffron, orange rind and herbs, tied in cheesecloth bag. Cook until almost all liquid has evaporated, 5 to 6 minutes.

Add tomato mixture to stock, and bring to boil over high heat. Reduce heat to low and simmer 10 minutes. Add shellfish and firm fish to stock and simmer 8 minutes. Add more delicate fish and simmer until fish flakes when tested with fork.

Season bouillabaisse with salt and pepper. To serve, arrange two toasted bread slices in each soup plate. Ladle bouillabaise over. Sprinkle each serving with 1 tablespoon parsley. Serve hot with *Rouille*.

FISH STOCK

1   pound fish bones, tails, heads and
        trimmings
1   medium onion, quartered
3   cloves garlic, mashed
1   small potato, pared and quartered
1   parsley sprig
1   bay leaf
1   sprig fresh thyme
1   sprig fresh fennel leaf

Bring 2½ quarts water in saucepan to boil over high heat. Reduce heat to medium low. Add fish trimmings, onion, garlic, potato and herbs tied in cheesecloth. Simmer until fish is tender and falls from bones, 10 to 15 minutes. Strain stock and return to saucepan. Reserve potato for rouille. Simmer stock, uncovered, until reduced to about 2 quarts, about 30 minutes.

ROUILLE

1/2   *sweet red pepper, seeded and chopped*
1   *teaspoon dried red pepper flakes*
4   *cloves garlic, peeled*
1   *tablespoon chopped fresh basil*
1/4   *cup olive oil*
1   *cooked potato (from stock)*
1/4   *cup Fish Stock*

Place red pepper and pepper flakes in small saucepan, and add just enough water to cover. Bring to simmer over medium heat. Simmer until tender, about 5 minutes. Drain. Place peppers, garlic, basil and oil in blender container or food processor work bowl fitted with steel blade. Blend or process until smooth. Add potato and stock. Blend or process until smooth.

NOTE: Fish can include: mussels, clams, crab, lobster, scallops, halibut, cod, pollock, grouper, sea bass, haddock, red snapper, trout, perch and lemon sole.

SOUPE À L'OIGNON GRATINÉE

Onion Soup

6 SERVINGS

2   *large Bermuda onions (1 1/2 pounds), peeled and thinly sliced*
2   *tablespoons butter*
2   *tablespoons vegetable oil*
1/2   *teaspoon sugar*
2   *tablespoons all-purpose flour*
7   *cups rich homemade beef broth*
1/2   *cup dry white wine*
1/2   *teaspoon Dijon mustard*
1/4   *teaspoon dried thyme, crumbled*
12   *slices French bread, 3/4 inch thick*
1 1/2   *cups (6 ounces) shredded Gruyère cheese*
6   *tablespoons freshly grated Parmesan cheese*

Sauté onions in butter and oil in a large covered saucepan or Dutch oven over medium-low heat, stirring frequently, until limp, about 15 minutes. Uncover and increase heat to medium. Stir in sugar. Cook, stirring frequently, until onions are a deep, golden brown, 40 to 45 minutes.

Sprinkle flour over onions. Cook, stirring constantly, about 3 minutes. Gradually stir in broth, wine, mustard and thyme. Increase heat to high and bring heat to boil. Reduce heat to low and simmer, partially covered, 35 to 40 minutes.

Arrange bread slices in single layer on baking sheet. Toast in preheated 325°F. oven until dry, about 30 minutes.

Ladle soup into heatproof serving bowls. Arrange 2 slices toasted bread over each bowl. Sprinkle each serving with 1/4 cup Gruyère and 1 tablespoon Parmesan. Broil 4 inches from heat until cheese is golden and bubbly, 2 to 3 minutes. Serve immediately.

COQUILLES ST. JACQUES

Scallops in White Wine
6 APPETIZER SERVINGS OR
4 ENTREE SERVINGS

1   cup dry white wine
1   tablespoon finely chopped shallots
½   bay leaf
1   pound fresh bay scallops
½   cup heavy cream
½   pound mushrooms, cleaned, trimmed
        and sliced
3   tablespoons butter
2   egg yolks
½   cup shredded Emmenthaler or Jarlsberg
        cheese
½   cup soft French bread crumbs
2   tablespoons butter, melted

Combine ⅔ cup wine, ⅓ cup water, shallots and bay leaf in 1½-quart saucepan. Bring to boil over high heat. Reduce heat to low, add scallops and poach just until white and firm, about 5 minutes. Remove scallops with slotted spoon. Strain liquid, return to saucepan and boil over high heat until reduced to ¼ cup. Stir in cream.

Sauté mushrooms in 3 tablespoons butter in medium skillet over medium-high heat until lightly browned, 6 to 8 minutes. Add remaining wine and cook until liquid evaporates. Butter 6 scallop shells and spread mushroom mixture evenly inside.

Bring reserved wine and cream mixture to simmer over medium heat. Reduce heat to low. Beat egg yolks with whisk in medium heat-proof bowl and gradually whisk in cream mixture. Return to saucepan and cook, stirring constantly, just until thickened, about 3 minutes. Stir in scallops.

Divide mixture evenly among shells and sprinkle with cheese. Toss bread crumbs with 2 tablespoons melted butter until mixed. Sprinkle evenly over cheese in shells (see Note).

Bake in preheated 500°F. oven until heated through, 8 to 10 minutes. Broil 4 inches from heat until lightly browned, about 1 minute. Serve immediately.

NOTE: Coquilles St. Jacques may be prepared several hours in advance to this point. Cover with plastic wrap and refrigerate until ready to serve. Increase baking time to heat thoroughly.

Shallots, fresh bay scallops, rich cream and sliced mushrooms are the savory ingredients of classic Coquilles St. Jacques.

BRIOCHE

Egg Bread

1 LARGE LOAF

4¼ cups all-purpose flour, plus additional
    ½ cup as needed
1   package active dry yeast (1 scant
    tablespoon)
12 tablespoons unsalted butter
½   cup milk
2   tablespoons sugar
1   teaspoon salt
4   eggs
1   egg yolk
½   to 1 cup (2 to 4 ounces) shredded
    Gruyère cheese (optional)
    Melted butter

Stir together 2 cups flour and yeast in large mixing bowl. Heat butter, milk, sugar and salt in small saucepan over low heat just until warm (115° to 120°F.). Add to flour mixture. Beat until smooth, about 2 minutes on medium speed of electric mixer or 300 strokes by hand. Beat in eggs, one at a time, beating well after each addition. Beat in egg yolk and cheese. Add 1 cup flour and beat 1 minute on medium speed or 150 strokes by hand. Stir in enough additional flour to make moderately stiff dough.

Turn dough onto lightly floured surface. Knead until smooth and satiny, 10 to 12 minutes. Shape into ball and place in lightly greased bowl, turning to grease all sides. Cover and let rise in warm place (80° to 85°F.) until doubled in bulk, about 1½ hours.

Punch dough down. Cover and let rest 10 minutes. Cut off about ⅕ of dough and shape into ball. Shape remainder into larger ball and place in greased 1½-quart brioche mold. Make depression about 1½ inches wide in center of dough. Insert smaller ball into depression. Brush dough with melted butter. Let rise in warm place until doubled in bulk, about 1 hour.

Bake in preheated 325°F. oven until bread is golden and sounds hollow when tapped, 35 to 40 minutes. Remove from pan immediately and place on wire rack. Brush with melted butter. Cool completely.

POIRES AU VIN ROUGE

Pears in Red Wine

6 SERVINGS

1   tablespoon fresh lemon juice
6   medium ripe, firm pears (preferably
    Bosc)

2   cups dry red wine
⅓   cup sugar
1   small stick cinnamon

1   strip (2 x ¼ inches) lemon rind
2   tablespoons Kirschwasser or cognac

Combine 2 cups water and lemon juice in large bowl. Peel pears and immediately immerse in water and lemon juice.

Bring wine, sugar, cinnamon and lemon rind to boil in 3- or 4-quart saucepan over medium-high heat. Add pears and bring to simmer. Reduce heat to low. Simmer, turning pears every 5 minutes, just until pears are tender when pierced with sharp knife, 10 to 15 minutes. Remove with slotted spoon and place in serving bowl.

Increase heat to high. Boil liquid until syrupy and reduced by half, 5 to 7 minutes. Remove from heat and stir in Kirschwasser. Discard cinnamon and lemon rind. Pour wine mixture over pears. Cover with plastic wrap and cool to room temperature. Refrigerate until thoroughly chilled, at least 2 hours. Serve cold.

ABOVE AND OVERLEAF: *Pears poached in red wine are a delightful close to any celebration.*

Personal victories and defeats have been recounted throughout this book. One still-unfolding story is that of Lee Iacocca, Chairman of The Statue of Liberty—Ellis Island Foundation. Iacocca was charged by President Reagan to spearhead the effort to raise private funds for the Ellis Island restoration.

His childhood memories recall his parents' steps through Ellis Island in establishing their roots in America. Today, he continues to enjoy the foods his mother, Antoinette, lovingly prepares. Of his mother's cooking, Iacocca's recent autobiography notes, "Of all the world's great Neapolitan cooks, she has to be one of the best."

Antoinette Iacocca offered us two of Lee's favorite recipes. They originally came from her mother and she brought them to America in 1921. We have reproduced them here in her own style.

NEAPOLITAN CANNELLONI

CREPES

1   cup flour
1   cup milk
4   eggs

Beat well—pour about ¼ cup of batter into small fry pan—turn—do not brown.

This should make about 20 crepes.

FILLING

1½ lbs. ricotta cheese
2   eggs
    Mozzarella cheese
    Salt and pepper
    Chopped parsley

Blend ricotta and eggs well.

In 9 x 12 baking dish—place on bottom a few cups of favorite home-made tomato sauce.

Place about a heaping tablespoon of ricotta mixture on crepe—place tiny narrow stick of mozzarella cheese on top—roll crepe—place open side down in single row on pan—add additional tomato sauce on top—sprinkle with grated cheese. Bake in slow 300° oven for 35 minutes.

MOM'S MEATBALL SOUP

MEATBALLS

1   lb. freshly ground veal
1   egg
1   tablespoon grated parmesan cheese
1   teaspoon chopped fresh parsley

Blend ingredients—form balls the size of a marble—add to 2 quarts of boiling home-made chicken broth. As broth starts to boil, add meatballs and simmer for 20 minutes. Sprinkle grated cheese and parsley on top.

page 1   Brown Brothers
page 13   Culver Pictures
page 17   Culver Pictures
page 18   Library of Congress
page 19   Culver Pictures
page 21   Brown Brothers
page 27   Lace runner courtesy Françoise Nunnalé, 105 West 55th Street, New York, New York
page 45   State Historical Society of Wisconsin/M. E. Diemer, photographer
page 46   Brown Brothers
page 47   Brown Brothers
page 48   State Historical Society of Wisconsin
page 49   Library of Congress/© 1904 Underwood and Underwood
page 66   Cake platter courtesy Hutchenreuther, 41 Madison Avenue, New York, New York
page 71   Library of Congress
page 75   Library of Congress
page 97   Culver Pictures
page 98   National Park Service/Statue of Liberty National Monument
page 99   Library of Congress
page 100   Brown Brothers
page 101   Brown Brothers
pages 102–103   Sterling silver tea service courtesy James Robinson Ltd., 15 East 57th Street, New York, New York Tablecloth courtesy Françoise Nunnalé, 105 West 55th Street, New York, New York
page 109   Crystal bowl courtesy James Robinson Ltd., 15 East 57th Street, New York, New York
page 123   National Park Service/Statue of Liberty National Monument
page 124   Liberty of Congress/R. F. Turnbull, photographer, 1900
page 125   Brown Brothers
page 126   Brown Brothers
page 127   New York Public Library/Lewis W. Hine, photographer
page 137   Gilded silver cream jug, ladle, salt chair, and gilded silver and enamel goblet courtesy A La Vielle Russie, 781 Fifth Avenue, New York, New York
page 149   Idaho Historical Society
page 151   Idaho Historical Society
page 153   Idaho Historical Society
page 157   Hand-thrown porcelain plate by Steven Stewart for Gordon Foster, 1322 Third Avenue, New York, New York
page 158   Portuguese plate by Steven Stewart for Gordon Foster, 1322 Third Avenue, New York, New York
pages 168–169   Tureen courtesy Gordon Foster, 1322 Third Avenue, New York, New York
page 171   Cheeses courtesy The Tapas Bar at the Rojas-Lombardi Restaurant at The Ballroom, 253 West 28th Street, New York, New York
page 175   Culver Pictures
page 177   Federal Art Project Changing New York, Museum of the City of New York/Berenice Abbot, photographer, 1937
page 178   Brown Brothers
page 179   Library of Congress/Lewis W. Hine, photographer
page 182   Tureen courtesy Hutchenreuther, 41 Madison Avenue, New York, New York
page 199   Culver Pictures
page 202   Library of Congress/Keystone View Company, B. L. Singley, photographer, 1904
page 203   Library of Congress/Keystone View Company, B.L. Single, photographer, 1904
page 225   National Archives
page 229   National Park Service/Statue of Liberty National Monument
page 235   Lace tablecloth courtesy Françoise Nunnalé, 105 West 55th Street, New York, New York
pages 248–249   Lace tablecloth courtesy Françoise Nunnalé, 105 West 55th Street, New York, New York

Antique tables throughout, courtesy Pierre Deux Antiques, 367–369 Bleecker Street, New York, New York

Flowers throughout, courtesy Very Special Flowers, 215 West 10th Street, New York, New York

Jacket, silver spoon courtesy Dworkin & Daughter.

ITALY

Gallo, Patrick J. *OLD BREAD, NEW WINE.* Chicago: Nelson-Hall, 1981.

Heaps, Willard A. *THE STORY OF ELLIS ISLAND.* New York: Seabury Press, 1964.

LaGumina, Salvatore J. *THE IMMIGRANTS SPEAK.* New York: Center for Migration Studies, 1979.

Lichine, Alexis. *ALEXIS LICHINE'S ENCYCLOPEDIA OF WINES AND SPIRITS.* New York: Alfred A. Knopf, 1967.

Root, Waverley, and Richard de Rochemont. *EATING IN AMERICA—A HISTORY.* New York: William Morrow and Co., 1976.

Scarpaci, Vincenza. *A PORTRAIT OF THE ITALIANS IN AMERICA.* New York: Charles Scribner's Sons, 1982.

Schiavo, Giovanni. *FOUR CENTURIES OF ITALIAN-AMERICAN HISTORY.* New York: Vigo Press, 1952.

GERMANY

Brown, Francis J., and Joseph S. Roucek. *OUR RACIAL AND NATIONAL MINORITIES.* New York: Prentice-Hall, 1937.

Furer, Howard B. *THE GERMANS IN AMERICA, 1607–1970.* Dobbs Ferry, New York: Oceana Publications, 1973.

Lichine, Alexis. *ALEXIS LICHINE'S ENCYCLOPEDIA OF WINES AND SPIRITS.* New York: Alfred A. Knopf, 1967.

Mitchell, Jan. *LUCHÖW'S GERMAN COOKBOOK.* New York: Doubleday and Co., 1952.

Morris, Richard B., and the editors of *LIFE. THE LIFE HISTORY OF THE UNITED STATES.* Vol. 1, *THE NEW WORLD.* New York: Time Incorporated, 1963.

Morrison, Joan, and Charlotte Fox Zabusky. *AMERICAN MOSAIC.* New York: New American Library, 1980.

O'Connor, Richard. *THE GERMAN-AMERICANS.* Boston: Little, Brown, and Co., 1968.

Rippley, LaVern. *THE GERMAN-AMERICANS.* Boston: Twayne Publishers, 1976.

Root, Waverley, and Richard de Rochemont. *EATING IN AMERICA—A HISTORY.*

New York: William Morrow and Co., 1976.

Schrader, Frederick Franklin. *THE GERMANS IN THE MAKING OF AMERICA.* Boston: Stratford Co., 1924.

Thernstrom, Stephen, et al, eds. *THE HARVARD ENCYCLOPEDIA OF AMERICAN ETHNIC GROUPS.* Cambridge, Massachusetts: Harvard University Press, 1980.

GREECE

Burgess, Thomas. *THE GREEKS IN AMERICA.* New York: Arno Press, 1970.

Chantiles, Vilma Liacouras. *THE FOOD OF GREECE.* New York: Atheneum, 1975.

Georgas, Demitra. "Greek Settlement of the San Francisco Bay Area." Master's thesis, University of California, Berkeley, 1951.

Lichine, Alexis. *ALEXIS LICHINE'S ENCYCLOPEDIA OF WINES AND SPIRITS.* New York: Alfred A. Knopf, 1967.

Miller, Wayne. *COMPREHENSIVE BIBLIOGRAPHY FOR THE STUDY OF AMERICAN MINORITIES.* New York: New York University Press, 1976.

Morrison, Joan, and Charlotte Fox Zabusky. *AMERICAN MOSAIC.* New York: New American Library, 1980.

Saloutos, Theodore. *THE GREEKS IN THE UNITED STATES.* Cambridge, Massachusetts: Harvard University Press, 1964.

Thernstrom, Stephen, et al, eds. *THE HARVARD ENCYCLOPEDIA OF AMERICAN ETHNIC GROUPS.* Cambridge, Massachusetts: Harvard University Press, 1980.

Xenides, J. P. *THE GREEKS IN AMERICA.* New York: Doran Publishing, 1922.

GREAT BRITAIN

Bolton, Charles. *SCOTCH IRISH PIONEERS IN ULSTER AND AMERICA.* Boston: Bacon and Brown, 1910.

Brown, Francis J., and Joseph S. Roucek. *OUR RACIAL AND NATIONAL MINORITIES.* New York: Prentice-Hall, 1937.

Coleman, Terry. *GOING TO AMERICA.* New York: Pantheon Books, 1972.

Colton, Calvin E., F. Westley, and A. H. Davis. *EMIGRANT'S MANUAL.* In *THE AMERICAN IMMIGRATION COLLECTION,* edited by Oscar Handlin. Series 1, 42 vols. New York: Ayer Co., 1969.

Considine, Bob. *IT'S THE IRISH.* New York: Doubleday and Co., 1961.

Conway, Alan, ed. *THE WELSH IN AMERICA.* Minneapolis: University of Minnesota Press, 1961.

Graham, Ian. *COLONISTS FROM SCOTLAND.* New York: Cornell University Press, 1956.

Levey, Judith S., and Agnes Greenhall, eds. *THE CONCISE COLUMBIA ENCYCLOPEDIA.* New York: Columbia University Press, 1983.

Morris, Richard B., and the editors of *LIFE. THE LIFE HISTORY OF THE UNITED STATES.* Vol. 1, *THE NEW WORLD.* New York: Time Incorporated, 1963.

———. *THE LIFE HISTORY OF THE UNITED STATES.* Vol. 2, *MAKING OF A NATION.* New York: Time Incorporated, 1963.

———. *THE LIFE HISTORY OF THE UNITED STATES.* Vol. 3, *THE GROWING YEARS.* New York: Time Incorporated, 1963.

Morrison, Joan, and Charlotte Fox Zabusky. *AMERICAN MOSAIC.* New York: New American Library, 1980.

Root, Waverly, and Richard de Rochemont. *EATING IN AMERICA—A HISTORY.* New York: William Morrow and Co., 1976.

Thernstrom, Stephen, et al, eds. *THE HARVARD ENCYCLOPEDIA OF AMERICAN ETHNIC GROUPS.* Cambridge, Massachusetts: Harvard University Press, 1980.

Todd, Arthur C. *THE CORNISH MINER IN AMERICA.* Truro, Cornwall: D. Bradford Barton, Ltd., 1967.

EASTERN EUROPE

Kuniczak, W. S. *MY NAME IS MILLION.* Garden City, New York: Doubleday, 1978.

Mocha, Frank, ed. *THE POLES IN AMER-*

ICA: BICENTENNIAL ESSAYS. Stevens Point, Wisconsin: Worzalla Publishing Co., 1978.

Morrison, Joan, and Charlotte Fox Zabusky. *AMERICAN MOSAIC.* New York: New American Library, 1980.

Root, Waverley, and Richard de Rochemont. *EATING IN AMERICA—A HISTORY.* New York: William Morrow and Co., 1976.

Thernstrom, Stephen, et al, eds. *THE HARVARD ENCYCLOPEDIA OF AMERICAN ETHNIC GROUPS.* Cambridge, Massachusetts: Harvard University Press, 1980.

IBERIA

Alford, Harold J. *THE PROUD PEOPLES.* New York: David McKay Co., 1972.

Brown, Francis J., and Joseph S. Roucek. *OUR RACIAL AND NATIONAL MINORITIES.* New York: Prentice-Hall, 1937.

Cardozo, Manoel da Silveira. *THE PORTUGUESE IN AMERICA, 590 B.C.–1974.* Dobbs Ferry, New York: Oceana Publications, 1976.

Hillman, Howard. *GREAT PEASANT DISHES OF THE WORLD.* Boston: Houghton Mifflin Co., 1983.

Lichine, Alexis. *ALEXIS LICHINE'S ENCYCLOPEDIA OF WINES AND SPIRITS.* New York: Alfred A. Knopf, 1967.

Pap, Leo. *THE PORTUGUESE AMERICANS.* Boston: G K Hall and Co., 1981.

Root, Waverley, and Richard de Rochemont. *EATING IN AMERICA—A HISTORY.* New York: William Morrow and Co., 1976.

Thernstrom, Stephen, et al, eds. *THE HARVARD ENCYCLOPEDIA OF AMERICAN ETHNIC GROUPS.* Cambridge, Massachusetts: Harvard University Press, 1980.

JEWISH

Benjamin, Robert, *ETHNIC HISTORIES: THE JEWISH IN AMERICA.* Chicago: Claretian Publications, 1972.

Brown, Francis J., and Joseph S. Roucek. *OUR RACIAL AND NATIONAL MINOR-*

ITIES. New York: Prentice-Hall, 1937.

Eisenberg, Azriel, ed., et al. *EYEWITNESSES TO AMERICAN JEWISH HISTORY: 1492–1793, PART ONE.* 4 vols. New York: Union of American Hebrew Congregations, 1976.

Gay, Ruth. *JEWS IN AMERICA.* New York, Basic Books: 1975.

Karp, Abraham. *GOLDEN DOOR TO AMERICA.* New York: Viking Press, 1976.

Lichine, Alexis. *ALEXIS LICHINE'S ENCYCLOPEDIA OF WINES AND SPIRITS.* New York: Alfred A. Knopf, 1967.

Morrison, Joan, and Charlotte Fox Zabusky. *AMERICAN MOSAIC.* New York: New American Library, 1980.

Root, Waverley, and Richard de Rochemont. *EATING IN AMERICA—A HISTORY.* New York: William Morrow and Co., 1976.

Schoener, Allon. *THE AMERICAN JEWISH ALBUM, 1654 TO THE PRESENT.* New York: Rizzoli International Publications, 1983.

Thernstrom, Stephen, et al, eds. *THE HARVARD ENCYCLOPEDIA OF AMERICAN ETHNIC GROUPS.* Cambridge, Massachusetts: Harvard University Press, 1980.

SCANDINAVIA

Barton, H. Arnold. *LETTERS FROM THE PROMISED LAND: SWEDES IN AMERICA, 1840–1914.* Minneapolis: University of Minnesota Press, 1975.

Furer, Howard B. *THE SCANDINAVIANS IN AMERICA, 986–1970.* Dobbs Ferry, New York: Oceana Publications, 1972.

Kastrup, Alan. *THE SWEDISH HERITAGE IN AMERICA.* St. Paul, Minnesota: Swedish Council of America, 1975.

Morrison, Joan, and Charlotte Fox Zabusky. *AMERICAN MOSAIC.* New York: New American Library, 1980.

Root, Waverley, and Richard de Rochemont. *EATING IN AMERICA—A HISTORY.* New York: William Morrow and Co., 1976.

Thernstrom, Stephen, et al, eds. *THE HARVARD ENCYCLOPEDIA OF AMERICAN*

ETHNIC GROUPS. Cambridge, Massachusetts: Harvard University Press, 1980.

FRANCE

Brown, Francis J., and Joseph S. Roucek. *OUR RACIAL AND NATIONAL MINORITIES.* New York: Prentice-Hall, 1937.

Caruso, John Anthony. *THE MISSISSIPPI VALLEY FRONTIER.* Indianapolis: Bobbs-Merrill, 1966.

Clarke, T. Wood. *EMIGRES IN THE WILDERNESS.* New York: Macmillan, 1941.

Finley, John. *THE FRENCH IN THE HEART OF AMERICA.* New York: Charles Scribner's Sons, 1915.

Gilder, Rodman. *STATUE OF LIBERTY ENLIGHTENING THE WORLD.* New York: New York Trust Co., 1943.

Idzerda, Stanley J. *FRANCE AND THE AMERICAN WAR FOR INDEPENDENCE.* New York: Scott Limited Editions, 1976.

Levey, Judith S., and Agnes Greenhall, eds. *THE CONCISE COLUMBIA ENCYCLOPEDIA.* New York: Columbia University Press, 1983.

Lichine, Alexis. *ALEXIS LICHINE'S ENCYCLOPEDIA OF WINES AND SPIRITS.* New York: Alfred A. Knopf, 1967.

McDermott, John Francis. *THE FRENCH IN THE MISSISSIPPI VALLEY.* Urbana: University of Illinois Press, 1965.

Morris, Richard B., and the editors of *LIFE. THE LIFE HISTORY OF THE UNITED STATES.* Vol. 1, *THE NEW WORLD.* New York: Time Incorporated, 1963.

———. *THE LIFE HISTORY OF THE UNITED STATES.* Vol. 2, *MAKING OF A NATION.* New York: Time Incorporated, 1963.

Root, Waverley, and Richard de Rochemont. *EATING IN AMERICA—A HISTORY.* New York: William Morrow and Co., 1976.

INDEX

Italic numbers indicate photographs.

Composed in Caslon Old Style and Cloister Open Face by TGA Communications Inc., New York, New York

Printed and bound by Amilcare Pizzi s.p.a.-arti grafiche, Milan, Italy